AUTUMN
GARDENS

AUTUMN
GARDENS

ETHNE CLARKE

PHOTOGRAPHS BY
JONATHAN BUCKLEY

David & Charles

A DAVID & CHARLES BOOK

First published in the UK in 1999
Copyright © David & Charles 1999
Text Copyright © Ethne Clarke 1999
Photographs Copyright © Jonathan Buckley 1999

A catalogue record for this book is available from
the British Library.

ISBN 0 7153 0701 0

Designed by Dick Malt

Printed in Singapore by C.S. Graphics Pte Ltd
for David & Charles
Brunel House, Newton Abbott, Devon

ACKNOWLEDGEMENTS

My sincerest thanks to Anna Mumford and her editorial team, for the support they gave me, Jonathan Buckley and Dick Malt in putting this book together – that we managed to do it across half a continent and the Atlantic Ocean is due in part to the wonders of e-mail, but mostly to Anna's faith in us and her willingness to just let us get on with it. I've worked with many editors, and she is one of the very best. We owe a huge debt of gratitude to the many garden owners who allowed us to include their gardens in this book; without their cooperation it would not have been possible to illustrate the special beauty of autumn.

Many of Jonathan's photographs were taken in gardens that have had an enormous influence on my development as a gardener – none more so than Mark Brown's garden in Normandy, France. He has a very light touch in the garden, and looks unfailingly to the native landscape for his inspiration He examines each flower in depth to understand its colour setting and the shape and texture of each leaf to help him discover its ideal partner. As a result, Mark's gardens, founded in harmony, transmit an almost spiritual tranquillity. Now I too try to look deeper, to understand as well as know my plants.

In Norfolk, England, Alan Gray and Graham Robeson have, from our very first meeting five or so years ago, demonstrated what it means to make a garden. When we first met they had not yet started opening their now quite famous garden, the Old Vicarage, East Ruston, to public view; I recall Alan saying that he wasn't sure anyone would want to see what they were doing! But when a garden is made with such conviction and such commitment to a single vision it stands as a beacon for what the creative process of garden-making is all about. Like all other art forms, it is highly personal, so if you are going to do it, do it for yourself and no one else. Follow your vision.

Having returned to live in the USA, my life has sort of come full circle. However, a new cycle is beginning. I learned my gardening in England, using a palette of plants that, by and large, would struggle to make a decent showing in my almost-tropical new garden. I am on the edge of two climate zones – 8 and 9 – and surrounded by limestone escarpments; the only way to garden realistically is with native plants or ones from parts of Mexico and Asia that share similar conditions – this I am learning from John Fairey at the Peckerwood Gardens near Houston (where he teeters on the brink of three climate zones!). While it is exciting to begin again at the bottom of the plant-learning curve, I will always value the skills and horticultural knowledge I gleaned from friends' gardens and from the many other beautiful gardens of Britain, too numerous to mention here, that I came to know and respect so highly.

It's been an interesting journey.

Ethne Clarke
Austin, Texas
March 1999

CONTENTS

INTRODUCTION

When I first considered writing a book on this subject, I lived in England and my inspiration came from the autumn character of my garden in rural Norfolk. Now, two years on, it is autumn once again, but I am living in south-central Texas and making an urban garden not far from downtown Austin. But there are echoes of my English autumn garden all around: the leaves of Chinaberry trees are turning egg yolk yellow and clustered in the fork of each branching bough are pendulous beads of tawny fruit, an image that brings to mind the rosy pink porcelain berries of the *Sorbus hupehensis* that I grew in my garden at Sycamore Barn. As Christmas approaches, I wonder what I will use in place of holly berries from the old field hedge for my seasonal decorations – probably sprays of Yaupon holly or maybe the coral fruit of *Nandina domestica*. In England, my most treasured autumn tree was *Liquidambar styraciflua*, so I am grateful to find that it grows well in Austin. The *Miscanthus* grasses and dwarf pampas that are so valuable for adding structure to

English autumn gardens serve the same purpose in subtropical Texas. During this season, gardeners everywhere are busily planting out pansies and early spring-flowering bulbs; sowing vegetable seed for second crops and early crops, and planning and planting perennial borders, shrubs and trees.

I can see that there are other similarities, but perhaps the most remarkable one of all is the way the warm days and cool nights in the Texas Hill Country produce soft hues of the sort you find in handwoven tweed, reminding me and expatriate English friends, of seasonal foliage in England and the Channel Islands. It might sound fanciful, but I can almost imagine myself back in Norfolk – were it not for the bright blue skies and temperatures around 30°C (the mid-80s Fahrenheit). In England we cherish the few sweet warm days of Indian summer when the temperature climbs back up before the winter cold sets in; I arrived in Texas in time to

LEFT *Contemplating autumn, many gardeners think first of the brightly coloured maples, like* Acer palmatum *'Sango-kaku', the most popular Japanese maple.*

ABOVE *Butterflies are attracted to autumn-flowering sedums.*

PREVIOUS PAGES *The foliage of a vine-covered tunnel in the Edwardian garden at Powis Castle frames the path in fiery tones.*
INSET *A contrast of shape and textures enhances the reflected glory of majestic pampas grass* (Cortaderia selloana) *and colourful sumac* (Rhus typhina).

experience the pleasurable few cool days that herald the onset of autumn. The symmetry ends with the climate.

Drought is another contributing factor to fine autumn colours – a dry summer season, no matter where you live, will enhance the tints of fading foliage. It will also have an impact on the plants we choose to grow, since gardeners everywhere are becoming more conscientious about the amount of fresh water they are willing to lavish on their gardens. When I gardened in East Anglia, Beth Chatto's dry garden was the prototype for a new approach to ecologically friendly horticulture. Careful soil preparation meant digging in quantities of rotted manure and compost to assist the moisture-retentive qualities of the planting zones. This was married to a highly selective choice of plants, focussing on only those which are suited to dry, free-draining conditions. Re-reading Beth's book, *The Dry Garden*, alongside Texan horticulturist Scott Ogden's *Gardening Success with Difficult*

Soils, I feel confident that the dry-gardening skills I learned in my English garden will be put to good use in Austin; general garden practice does not alter no matter where you live.

DIG THAT GARDEN

Autumn is unquestionably the busiest time of the gardening year. Digging features as the main activity (so it is time to brush up on relaxing exercises to relieve strained muscles, and stock up on Epsom salts for soothing baths). New beds and planting zones can be prepared, established perennials lifted and divided as they die back, seed gathered for propagation, or root and stem cuttings taken to increase stocks. Don't be in too much of a hurry to 'tidy up' or you risk depriving yourself of some of autumn's glory in the faded seedheads and foliage dotting the flower garden. However, do make good time while the sun shines to do the digging.

Tilling the soil is a gardener's most fundamental activity; you can't garden if you don't dig. Some people, including myself, could wish this was otherwise; too much energetic spadework in the early years of garden-making has left me with a back and shoulders that squeal in anguish at the onset of autumn – but maybe it's the weather not the sight of the spade. But, as in all things in life, there are levels of commitment to this activity and there are ways to almost, but not quite, avoid it altogether.

We dig to loosen the soil, to incorporate nutrients and to improve drainage, thereby making it easier for the plants we grow to thrive in the artificial environment of the garden. The best time of year to dig is autumn, because then the rain

ABOVE *Autumn is known as the season of mists and mellow fruitfulness. The soft moist air and low light at this time of year create special effects in the garden that can be exploited by the observant gardener.*

and freezes of winter will further break down the overturned clods of earth, making it easier to create a fine tilth in spring when it is time to plant and sow.

There are different levels of digging: single digging, where you turn over one spade-blade of soil only, and confine the

Single digging, however, will do the trick for most gardens where new planting areas are being prepared or old ones revitalized. This type of manual cultivation involves nothing greater than digging to one spade depth, incorporating the compost that has been first spread evenly and generously over the surface of the area being worked.

Pace yourself and dig only the amount you can comfortably lift on the spade. Use a well-made spade too, one with a good sharp edge and that has its top edges rolled or shaped where your foot is placed to help you push the blade into the soil. Hold the spade upright as the blade bites into the soil, then slide whichever hand is not on the handle down the shaft, bend your knees slightly to take the strain off your lower back, and gently turn the clod of soil over. Work rhythmically and pause when necessary to straighten your back. Also, holding the spade with the hand nearest the blade on top of the shaft in an overhand grip, seems to balance the push-pull action of digging. Experiment until you find what best suits your ability. And always remember that Rome wasn't built in a day.

So, take time out to enjoy the glow of the autumn sun as it warms your back and shoulders, pause to admire the crisp clouds scuttering across the sky and enjoy the company of the ever-inquisitive robins and blackbirds that will be close at hand to pluck any tasty morsel from the path of your spade.

disturbance to the top 20–25cm (8–10in) of soil, and double digging, which involves removing soil to a depth of at least two spade-blades so that you will probably be digging into the subsoil.

Double digging is only really necessary if you are preparing a previously uncultivated site – like the garden of a newly built house – because it breaks up compacted soils, allows the compost to be incorporated at deep-root level, assists the removal of deep-rooting perennial weeds and greatly improves the drainage of water-retentive areas.

THE SHAPE
OF AUTUMN

There are many interesting phenomena by which we mark the passing of the seasons and one of the most curious occurs only when weather conditions combine to provide a sunny day when the breeze is light enough to stir the colouring leaves and the temperature is warm, but which by evening has dropped to a brisk coolness. On days such as these zillions of baby spiders hatch, to be carried far away from home by the breeze catching up their infant spinner threads and depositing them on branches, lawns, garden furniture and the wilting forms of later summer perennials. The next day, in the early morning, be sure to walk out into the dew-covered garden and you will clearly see a spidery shroud mantling everything, as each silken filament edged in moisture forms a silvery tissue of gossamer thread. Natural events such as this are the mark of autumn – a season that is cherished for its moments of unsullied beauty and for the pleasure to be had from the commonplace garden activities that mark its passing.

The weather at this time of year is often unsettled and so you will have to make the most of sunny, clement days since digging and general autumn chores like leaf-raking and mulching can't be done in the rain. You should avoid, too, working on beds and planting areas after heavy rain as the wet soil will compact under the weight of your footsteps.

Pay attention to your compost heaps. Like clean shirts, every gardener should have at least two, if not three – one in use, one in readiness and one brand new. Having said that, I always managed with two (compost heaps, that is). All the vegetable waste from the kitchen went into one, as well as leaves, grass clippings, shredded newspaper, vacuum cleaner fluff and dust bunnies, twiggy branches and annual weeds pulled from around the garden – but no perennial weeds to pollute the heap. To this was added a leavening of an occasional spadeful of soil and compost activator – nitrogen-rich chicken manure from my little community of hens. When one bin was full it would be left to rot down while the next was being filled.

The counsel of perfection is that the heap should be built in careful layers, turned regularly so the outer edges exchange places with the inner layers; it should be kept covered and watered, if and when it dries out. I'm sure that such scientifically tended heaps produce Premium Grade compost, but the stuff that came out of the corner of the kitchen garden seemed to do the trick, even if it was not completely rotted down and traces of smashed egg shell and old teabags remained to sully its brown crumbly bulk. One of the most rudimentary methods of composting was practised in the vegetable patch of my uncle Joe's garden in Ireland; Pat, the gardener, simply dug in the day's vegetable waste directly into the section of garden which was laying fallow, on the principle of making it easier for the worms to get to it, 'which is why they bury us so deep, you know'. It surely made me aware of the importance of compost, of any kind, as a soil conditioner.

Except in areas where winter comes very early, it is generally recognized that autumn is the prime season for planting;

ABOVE *Back-lighting emphasizes the sinuous frame of* Acer palmatum *var.* dissectum *Dissectum Atropurpureum Group.*

RIGHT *The bright autumn colour of deciduous trees highlights the strong shapes of evergreens like the weeping habit of* Chamaecyparis nootkatensis *and the glaucous needles of a Colorado blue spruce.*

PREVIOUS PAGES *Autumn accents the broad-spreading crown of the colourful, spring-flowering cherry,* Prunus *'Shirotae'.*
INSET *Dew-laden cobwebs span the branches in autumn gardens.*

the soil is warm from summer, there are occasional rainfalls and this encourages transplanted trees and shrubs to produce new growth to help them settle easily into their new quarters. Even during winter, when top growth is slowed or killed by freezing weather, underground the roots will continue to grow – and a good insulating blanket of mulch 5–7.5cm (2–3in) thick, applied in early autumn, will ensure that this is so.

TREES

Trees are the foundation of the landscape, without their presence the garden picture would sprawl before us – trees anchor their companions to the site and arrest our vision. During autumn, this fact is at its most apparent; the often-times startling colour of deciduous foliage that precedes leaf-drop is followed by the drama of twisted branches and gnarled trunks. Evergreen trees, too, are more evident in the landscape as their dark mass and solid shapes are thrown into chiaroscuro relief against the nakedness of their garden companions. In the summertime, however, deciduous and evergreen trees fill in the background of summer flower borders and colourful spring shrubs; if we are aware of them at all it is for the shadows they cast.

In 1930, the American landscape architect, Jens Jensen, stated that the building blocks of a garden were 'the contours of the earth, the vegetation that covers it, the changing season, the rays of the setting sun, and the afterglow, and the light of the moon', and admonished all garden-makers to work with the natural landscape, using its characteristics as guides to plant choices and composition. This principle is one sure way of successfully finding your way through the myriad number of beautifully-leaved trees until you find the one that must be included in your autumn garden scheme.

Study the native trees in the landscape around your area and select the genus that for you has the most autumnal appeal. Expand on the native plant theme by researching species or cultivars within the same genus; you may find alternatives that have more showy foliage, bark or other decorative attribute but which would still suit your garden's habitat.

Consider, too, the nature of the tree's appeal. Is it just leaf colour that holds your attention, or will the foliage shape and texture add to the garden picture during the rest of the year? It may be that the bark has a highly individual character, which can be made more of by heeding the final words of Jensen's statement. Exploit the light in your garden – sunlight and moonlight – by placing a specimen tree or trees where the foliage will be illuminated or the bark highlighted by the special quality of autumn light as it falls in your garden. All gardeners know that they should familiarize themselves with patterns of light and shadow in their gardens, so that they know the different planting areas. But aside from this practical aspect of light and shade is the appreciation of the quality of natural light; how the glow of the rising sun slowly heats the eastern aspect of the garden and how the low angle of the setting sun sends rivers of shadow flowing across a lawn. Depending upon the atmosphere of the garden, the light can give a peach or violet tint to the scene, but this is a transient effect and not one which can play too big a part in garden planting plans.

Most trees respond well to autumn planting; there are exceptions, among them fleshy rooted subjects such as tulip trees (*Liriodendron tulipifera*) and magnolias. Some evergreens too, need protection if planted in the autumn; and in any case most should be planted in the early part of the season. But most of the favourite trees for autumn colour, such as *Acer* (maple trees), *Cornus* (dogwoods), *Quercus* (oaks) and *Prunus* (cherry trees), will do well planted in the autumn since all these trees begin to go dormant as soon as the soil starts to cool. Their energy is conserved in the roots during this time and is not being utilized to provide top growth.

Trees are available from nurseries either bare-rooted (which is not exactly an accurate description as the root ball will be wrapped in burlap or hessian), or container-grown. Large specimen trees are generally lifted mechanically from tree nurseries once all their leaves have dropped; container-grown plants tend to be smaller, anything from juvenile saplings to more mature trees with trunk diameters up to 5–7.5cm (2–3in). Unless you need an instant effect, it is often not worth the extra expense of purchasing large trees (which really are best dealt with by professional arborists). It seems to take five years for a tree to settle into its new home, no matter what its size when transplanted, and once it has got its toes into the soil, a sapling will grow away more rapidly than its more mature companions and have caught up by its eighth or ninth year. The only essential requirement is patience on the part of the gardener.

Just like general digging in the garden, digging planting holes for trees requires some small degree of method. Have ready a sharp spade and fork, a stake at least 1–1.2m (3–4ft) long, tree ties and sharp secateurs. The planting hole must be at least 30–60cm (1–2ft) bigger in diameter than the tree's root ball or container size. Slope the sides of the planting hole rather than making them straight up and down, and make the hole irregular in shape, rather than a perfect circle, to encourage the new root system to spread outwards. The hole should only be as deep as the tree was in the nursery ground or container; you can discern this by looking at the trunk – the 'nursery line' will be a mark on the bark where the dark, below-soil-level section of the trunk meets the light, above-soil-level section. Plant a little high to allow for settling.

Use the fork to loosen the base and to aerate the sides of the hole. Fill it with water, and while this is absorbed, turn your attention to the tree. Always carry the tree by the pot or transport it in a wheelbarrow; don't lug it around by the trunk as the weight of the soil-laden root ball puts enormous strain on the roots. Remove the container or wrapping and inspect the roots. Cut away any that are damaged or withered, but no more than this. If the root ball is congested or circling around on itself, tease it out with your fingers.

Place the tree in the hole, positioning it so its best aspect can be viewed from one particular vantage point if that is how it fits into your plan, and generally taking care that it is upright and not listing to one side or the other, and that you are satisfied with the place you have assigned it in the garden. It is easier to move perennials and shrubs that are, after time,

in the wrong place than it is to move a tree, so endeavour to get it right the first time.

Back-fill with a few spades of soil to hold the tree steady while you put in the stake. Large specimen trees require back-hoes, guy ropes and hawsers to plant and stake, which is why I stated earlier that their handling is best left to professional arborists. But for the average nursery stock tree in a 5l (1gal) container, an oak tree stake is sufficient. Place it on the side of the tree which faces the prevailing wind about 5cm (2in) from the base of the tree; pound it into the base of the planting hole until it feels securely embedded. The stake does not need to extend any higher than 30–45cm (12–18in) above ground; some gardeners advocate stakes tall enough to reach the lowest branch of the young tree – up to 60–100cm (2–3ft) – but short-staking allows the tree to sway and move in the wind and this movement encourages a stronger root system to develop more quickly to anchor the tree in its new home. Put the tree tie in place; most come with a spacer collar so that the tie is fixed in a figure of eight and the tree is held securely but not strangled by the tie. Old nylon tights, strips of plastic bag and lengths of rope just *will not* do; not only are they unsightly, they can harbour pests and damage the bark by constant abrasion and will not allow for growth as the tree trunk puts on girth.

Back-fill the planting hole, breaking up the clods of earth as you go. When the task is nearly complete, tread the soil in gently around the base of the tree to firm the soil around the roots. It is not necessary to add any compost, manure or fertilizer to the soil when planting trees; the goal is to have

ABOVE *The view across the terraces at Dinmore Manor, Hereford-shire, is transformed by the bold colourings of autumn in plants such as the Japanese maples and Virginia creeper dominating the scene.*

CENTRE *Even the veil of autumn mist can hold back the colour of a Japanese maple. These trees take on every shade of red, orange and yellow to dark purple and are essential to the autumn garden.*

RIGHT *Two sorts of* Enkianthus, E. campanulatus *in the foreground and* E. cernuus f. rubens *in the background, demonstrate the variation in autumn colour to be found among plants in the same genus.*

the tree establish itself quickly by sending out feeder roots and if the food is within easy reach, the roots will not fan out into the surrounding soil.

After planting the tree, water it well to settle it in the soil; if the season is dry, water at least once a week right up until the first freeze. If you berm the soil around the planting hole, it creates a small well which can be filled with water that will trickle down to the roots rather than run off into the surrounding area.

The only pruning that should be done at this stage is to remove weak twiggy growth along the main trunk and to cut out any damaged branches. Also, if there are any crossing branches, cut away the one which contributes least to the overall shape of the crown, and if there is a double leader (the main upward growing shoot), prune away the weakest.

Finally, top off with a good blanket of mulch around the foot of the tree, but keep the mulch out of direct contact with the trunk. Most deciduous trees can withstand winter conditions, but evergreen trees planted in autumn may need to be screened with horticultural fabric to avoid desiccation by winter winds. There are spray-on anti-desiccants that give

foliage a protective coating to minimize moisture loss, but these must re-applied weekly to have any effect.

SHRUBS

As I wrote in my book *Leaf, Bark and Berry*, the landscape appears in layers, and beneath the canopy of trees is the understorey, inhabited by shrubs, perennials, annuals and biennials (the ephemeral layer) and groundcover.

Shrubs are the walls of the garden, filling the space beneath trees and shaping our view of the landscape. By creating windows framed by ornamental foliage, our vision is directed outward or the surrounding landscape is drawn into the garden. As hedging, shrubs block the distant view to create an inward-looking realm.

Evergreen shrubs are most often used to create barrier hedges since their foliage is permanent; the shade they cast also becomes a permanent feature of the garden, and it diffi-

cult to grow anything below their dark mass. Deciduous shrubs, on the other hand, admit the warmth and moisture that the perennial and ephemeral layer requires during the growing season. Groupings of deciduous shrubs selected for their mutual growing requirements of sun or shade, acid or alkaline soil, moist or dry ground make a significant addition to the garden all year round since many have highly decorative flowers, delicious perfumes, elegant habits of growth, showy bark and brilliant colour.

One of my favourite all-round shrubs, that lacks only fragrance, is *Viburnum plicatum* 'Mariesii'. It holds its branches in graceful spreading tiers, and in summer they are clothed along their uppermost edges with pale white flowers like tiny saucers balancing on a table edge. The long oval leaves droop down either side of the branches and in autumn they turn a rich burgundy-red before dropping to reveal the spreading structure of the shrub. But as is often the case, there is another species within the genus that, being upright-growing, offers a pleasing though completely different habit, and has richly scented flower clusters in early spring and glowing vinous tones in autumn: *V.* × *bodnantense* 'Dawn'. Cutting branches of this shrub for indoor decoration during late winter and early spring ensures that there will be plenty of new growth to produce flowers the following year.

Unlike trees which can stand as solitary specimens in a garden scheme, shrubs appear best in groups. This was recognized by William Robinson who was one of the earliest English garden writers to advocate the use of mixed perennial and shrub borders to create natural habitats for less common and 'difficult' flowering plants. At his home, Gravetye Manor in Sussex, Robinson exercised his theories. He wrote of his experience in several books, most notably *The English Flower Garden*, and a journal on the development of Gravetye. Of shrub planting he wrote that he liked to plant 'in bold beds to screen rather steep and awkward banks, and at the same time to give a home to many fine things that would not be very well placed in the flower garden.' He advised that the edge of a shrub planting should be sinuous, undulating and irregular and that tall-growing flowers and bulbs like lilies should be worked in along the foremost edges to give a soft and pleasing line.

Mixed shrub borders are not without their maintenance chores, and chief among these is the need to prune carefully to thin out and to some degree sculpt the shrubby bulk into pleasing forms so that each plant clearly retains its identity. Left untended, shrubs have a way of growing together into a large homogeneous mass. Otherwise, planting a shrub is much the same as planting a tree, except that the shrub will not require any staking.

CLIMBERS

One of the plants which most readily leaps to mind when thinking of autumn colour is *Parthenocissus quinquefolia*, which is popularly known as Virginia creeper. The archetypal memory many of us share of this plant is of vivid crimson leaves cloaking the burnished masonry of hallowed halls, like those of Harvard and Yale and the other 'Ivy League' universities of New England – a region which is itself regarded as being at the epicentre of Fall Colour. Its relative, *P. henryana* is more subtle in its autumn finery, but just as decorative, with the silvery white veins on the leaflets becoming more pronounced as the foliage darkens to ruby red. These plants climb by means of adhesive tendrils; each little filament ends in a suckering pad that sticks to the support. To begin with they need some guidance to start the upward climb, but once settled in will begin their attachment to the support. For this reason it is often advised not to grow ivy against brick or stone walls because the suckering action is thought to erode the mortar – although some pundits disagree thinking the ivy

RIGHT *Optimize the autumn light in your garden by arranging plants so that their foliage will be illuminated. Here the familiar shape of the purple-leaved grape,* Vitis vinifera *'Purpurea', is accented by the glow of autumn afternoon sun, and the red foliage of orach,* Atriplex hortensis *var.* rubra, *plays off the purple colouring.*

LEFT *The sight of this naturalized patch of the Japanese anemone,* Anemone × hybrida *'Honorine Jobert', would warm the heart of William Robinson, whose book* The Wild Garden *promoted planting herbaceous perennials at the woodland edge to give a more relaxed and natural atmosphere to the garden. He also compiled* The English Flower Garden *in which he described this Japanese anemone as, 'a beautiful plant; and all good forms of the plant should be cultivated where cut flowers are required in autumn. By having some on a north border, and some on a warm one, the bloom may be prolonged. [They are also] useful for groups, fringes of shrubbery in rich soil, and here and there in half-shady places by wood walks.'*

ABOVE *A woodland path, winding along the edge of a small lake at The Dingle in Wales is framed with grey-barked eucalyptus and a wide variety of confetti-coloured shrubs and small trees.*

RIGHT *Elsewhere in the same garden, mop-headed hydrangeas toss their wine-stained bracts into the background foliage of the service berry,* Amelanchier canadensis.

offers a protective cloak, so the jury remains out on that question. The evergreen English ivy, *Hedera helix*, is most often accused of this.

Members of the grape vine genus, *Vitis*, also give rich autumn colouring, and there are few climbers more vibrant than *Vitis coignetiae*. It has enormous heart-shaped leaves that turn to shades of orange, red and yellow as autumn advances. It is a rampant climber and, like ivy, will quickly cover a supporting wall – but then go on to consume the

building. Grape vines climb by curly tendrils that emerge at the leaf axil, snaking out in curving arcs until they find something to wrap around; if you study the direction of the curl, you can sometimes assist this process by wrapping the tendrils in the correct direction around the support.

Akebia quinata is much loved by Japanese gardeners for the delicacy of its evergreen foliage; it is a dainty plant with tiny leaflets and lantern-like flowers. This is a twining climber, it wraps around the support in a tangle of sinuous stems.

Climbing roses are the best examples of climbers which use their thorns like grappling hooks to gain a purchase on the support. Other woody stemmed climbers, like blackberries, rely on thorns as their stems are not designed to twine. Even so, the long canes need guidance and should be pruned and tied into the support in an organized fashion to avoid an ungainly tangle. However, some roses, like *Rosa* 'Rambling Rector', can be left to their own devices to scramble through

trees casting their flowers and autumn clusters of dusky hips through the tree crown.

In small gardens, where shrubs as understorey fillers might take up too much space, climbers can take their place, providing a foliage background for flower borders or a screen to direct or frame the view. If a permanent wall of foliage is required, select one of the evergreen climbers like *Euonymus fortunei*, perhaps 'Variegatus' with white and yellow striations on the leathery leaves, or a berried evergreen such as one chosen from among the pyracanthas.

If constant cover is not an issue, then the selection is wide open as there are many deciduous climbers to provide colourful autumn backgrounds. One thing to bear in mind when making a choice is how much space you are going to allow the plant, and how much time you want to spend keeping it under control. Unlike the metabolism of a tree or shrub which is geared to making solid supportive woody growth, most climbers use all their energy to climb, which is why their growth remains supple. So they tend to be quite vigorous; when new growth begins in early spring is the time to begin training and thinning while the wood is still supple and before the climbing gets out of control.

Climbers can also be trained horizontally to form ground-cover, although the tendency will always be there to begin climbing any vertical object they bump into. However, a small-leaved grape vine like *Vitis* 'Brant' or an annual ornamental bean like *Lablab purpureus*, or hycacinth bean, would be manageable in this situation.

The type of support you select for a climber is to some extent determined by its method of climbing. One of the neatest, most efficient supports is made of aluminium wire stretched between vine eyes to form a square grid; the minimum distance between the wires, vertically and horizontally, is 10cm (4in), and the vine eyes should be long enough to

leave at least a 10cm (4in) gap between the wall and the wire. Tendril climbing plants will do well on wire trellis; additionally it has the advantage of permanence over wooden trellis, that will eventually rot unless treated regularly, which means removing the climber. Roses which are trained annually and climbers which are heavily pruned after flowering can be trained against a wooden grid since the pruning allows an opportunity for trellis maintenance.

When planting a climber always position it at least 30–40cm (12–18in) away from the support and position the root ball at a tilt in the planting hole so that the top growth is angled towards the support. This rule of distance is important to observe especially when the climber is grown against a wall; the soil near the foot of the wall will be much drier and less fertile as foundation material leaches out water and can release undesirable minerals or chemicals. Digging a planting hole this distance from the base of a tree trunk will be less likely to interfere with the tree's root system. Nevertheless, in this circumstance the climber will be competing with the tree for nourishment, so give the climber a regular foliar feed during the growing season to provide an extra boost; once it is established it should be able to fend for itself.

Make the planting hole large enough to accommodate the root ball and, as most climbers are greedy feeders, add a

LEFT *Autumn colouring vines include the widely known and grown Virginia creeper,* Parthenocissus quinquefolia *and* P. tricuspidata, *or Boston ivy. Both vines colour ruby red in autumn, and make a splendid contrast to evergreen English ivy,* Hedera helix.

handful of bone meal or slow-release general fertilizer to the back-fill. If the roots are compacted in the container, tease them out gently with your fingers or a hand-fork. Spread them evenly in the hole and then firm in some soil to hold the plant in position while you guide it against the support, and secure in place with a loose tie. Then finish filling the hole, firming the soil around the plant with your heel. Water the plant regularly until it is established and keep it mulched to conserve moisture in the soil.

PERENNIALS FOR GROUNDCOVER

There are many prostrate and carpeting perennial plants that will provide excellent groundcover throughout the growing season and well into autumn. Some offer coloured foliage all the year round and so make useful contrasts beneath shrubs and perennials during summer and then tone in with the autumn colour of their neighbours as the seasons change.

Harmonious autumn schemes based on yellow could be devised using groundcovers like golden marjoram, bright yellow lemon balm or yellow-variegated periwinkles beneath yellow-stemmed dogwood (*Cornus stolonifera* 'Flaviramea') in company with the yellow autumn colour of the birch *Betula maximowicziana*. The full show might last only as long as the birch holds its leaves, but the dogwood and the periwinkle would go on well into winter.

In her book, *Groundcover Plants*, Margery Fish described how silver foliage complements red- and bronze-leaved plants like the purple form of smoke bush, *Cotinus coggygria*. Conversely, purple bugle, *Ajuga reptans* 'Atropurpurea', would make a splendid wine-red carpet beneath a silver-leaved *Artemisia* like *A.* 'Powis Castle'. Artemisias have some of the best silver foliage going; *A. ludoviciana* 'Silver Queen' is nearly white and creeps around by underground stems. So does *A. pontica*, but give this one a wide berth unless you have plenty of space, as in good soil it quickly forms an impenetrable mat of stems. It has a dull pewter colour and frothy texture, and Margery Fish describes seeing it carpet the ground beneath apple trees in an orchard.

Before planting an area with groundcover, be sure it is clear of perennial weeds; competition for moisture and nutrients must be kept to a minimum and unsightly weeds would spoil the cohesiveness of the groundcover carpet. The planting distances depend upon the size and vigour of the groundcover plant: generally speaking the smaller the plant the closer the spacing, so a dwarf carpeting thyme would be spaced at 10–15cm (4–6in) centres, while larger more rampant plants like *Lamium* could be further apart at 25–30cm (10–12in). Make the plantings in an irregular pattern rather than rigid straight lines, unless you desire a formal rhythm to the scheme.

Groundcover beneath deciduous shrubs and trees should be swept to remove fallen leaves, as collected debris encourages disease and causes the groundcover to die off in unsightly patches. Trailing groundcovers like periwinkle can be sheared back to keep their growth in check and dwarf herbs like thyme can be gone over with a strimmer/weed-whacker or garden shears to keep growth tight and to remove flowerheads in late summer.

LAWNS

Probably the most universally popular groundcovering plant is grass; more hours are spent looking after grass lawns than any other part of the garden in the quest for the perfect greensward. And most of those hours are exhausted in autumn. There is no question that an even green carpet is the perfect setting for colourful and varied plantings at any time of year, and as with all things, perfection begins with thorough preparation.

New lawns grown from seed establish best in the cool days and nights of autumn when rainfall is more frequent, helping to make germination more even; try to time seed-sowing to six to eight weeks before the first frosts in your area. The type of seed mix you choose will be dependant upon the climate in your area, the amount of wear and tear the lawn will receive, and the appearance you wish to achieve.

Lawns do best on level ground in full sun, so use a shade-loving evergreen groundcover beneath trees and on sloping ground. Begin by clearing the site, removing all perennial weeds and scraping off annual weeds with a sharp spade. If the area to be sown is thick with weeds, use a herbicide during the summer when the weeds are growing strongly. It may take several applications for total annihilation, but the dead growth can be incorporated into the soil before sowing since the ground must be dug over to at least a spade's depth. Then rake or use a roto-tiller to break the soil down to a fine tilth, adding well-rotted manure or compost as you go. Grass does best on nearly neutral soil, so test the pH – if it is acid (low reading) add lime to the soil; if alkaline (high pH), dust the ground with sulphur.

Firm the seedbed by close-treading the ground or by using a lawn roller; aim for as level a surface as possible and take care not to compact the soil while firming. If possible, leave the soil to settle for a week or two (and for any errant weeds to appear) before sowing the seed. If the soil has dried out more than 2.5cm (1in) deep, water the ground first. Then use a lawn spreader or else scatter the seed by hand in slow even arcs; first in one direction using half the seed, and then go back over the ground at right angles to your first pass until all the seed is gone. If you are methodical you should achieve an even cover. Tread the seed in by walking diagonally across the newly sown area, and then water lightly and regularly until the seed germinates; use a fine misting spray on a hose attachment rather than a sprinkler – the regular mechanical pattern will wash the seed out of the soil. Set out a scarecrow or else stretch humming tape across the newly sown lawn to protect it from birds, and cordon it off to keep children and pets from walking on it until the first mowing, which can be done when the young grass is about 7.5cm (3in) high. Set the mower blades high for the first clip and be sure they are freshly sharpened. Subsequent mowings can be made quite close to encourage the grass to bulk up.

If an entirely new lawn is not required, but the existing lawn is looking ragged in patches, use turf to replace the unsightly parts. Autumn is also the best time to establish turf-laid lawns and repairs. Prepare the planting site just as carefully as for a seed-sown lawn.

To repair a small area, just remove the existing turf, gently break up the surface of the soil with a sharp border fork and lay the turfs in place, butting them up tightly against each other and then trim to fit with a sharp knife. Water in well.

Entire lawns laid from turf are not complicated to do; prepare the soil as above in advance of the turf being delivered from the nursery; the idea is to get the lawn laid quickly as the longer the turf is stacked the more it will dry out and turn yellow from lack of light. You will need a plank to walk on as you work and a taut garden line stretched across the area as a guide. Lay the first line of turfs, sprinkling compost between the 'seams' so that they will knit together as the grass grows. Move the plank onto this line of turf, then lay the next row so that the seams of the second row alternate with the seams of the first row, just as bricks are laid in a wall. The key to success is watering, so don't let the turf dry out. In the cool autumn weather the individual turfs will soon grow together to form a healthy green carpet.

PRAIRIES AND SUMMER MEADOWS

Many gardeners, in their quest for the natural, are rethinking the lawn as a design component, seeking to better complement the more relaxed style of naturalized perennial plantings. In the United States, prairie lawns are increasing in popularity, while in the UK, meadow lawns are featuring in contemporary schemes.

Some gardenmakers, too, feel that a lawn lacks the romance of the prairie; a recitation of the names of the many native species of grass and flowering perennial, or forb, that populate a true prairie lawn becomes a seductive mantra. Big

bluestem and little bluestem, indiangrass, rosinweed, sweet black-eyed Susan, rattlesnake master, compassplant, and prairie blazingstar are a few of the many species that once carpeted the Midwestern Plains of the USA, but soon vanished beneath the sodbuster's plough during the great expansions of the nineteenth century. English meadows, once rich with oxlips, primroses, snakeshead fritillaries, lady's slipper orchids, cuckoo flowers, purple self-heal and other flowering herbs, have all but disappeared beneath the mechanized farming methods of the industrial age.

The swing towards 'wild gardening' follows on the heels of increasing ecological awareness wherever people garden. However, not everyone is prepared to convert wholeheartedly to this innovative aesthetic; tradition dies hard and well-manicured gardens and lawns have long been most people's ideal – even when it comes with a high-maintenance price-tag. That is not to say the prairies and meadows are not without their care regimes, but the mowing involved happens once or twice a year, rather than each week. Most beneficially, however, herbicides are not required, and the flowery carpet

LEFT *Throughout the year, contrasts of shape are as important as contrasts of colour to heighten visual impact, and some perennials offer foliage that is consistently interesting like this lungwort,* Pulmonaria saccharata, *the silver markings accented by the white blooms of the autumn-flowering* Clematis × jouiniana *'Praecox'.*

RIGHT *Similarly, bright green* Euphorbia mellifera *seen against a backdrop of the vine* Vitis *'Brant' will be attractive all year round.*

becomes a refuge for wildlife; birds and insects find the seeds and nectar they need to survive and the benefits to local ecology will be seen in a greatly expanded biodiversity.

Prairie and meadow patches can be a part of a conventional garden design – no need to sweep away the perennial borders and roses – by setting aside a piece of ground, perhaps a circular bed in the centre of a sun-filled yard framed by a gravel path, or a ribbon of ground along a driveway. By late summer or early autumn, the flowering plants are in their prime and the grasses begin making a show of ripening seedheads.

Apart from starting with a clear site, planting the prairie lawn needs a little forward planning. Six weeks prior to early summer sowing, the seed, mixed with sand, must be stratified by storing in the refrigerator – this is essential to the

LEFT *When shrubs and perennials cohabit in a mixed border, give a thought to the effect they will have on each other throughout the year – not just in summer. In the border at Abbey Dore, the pampas grass* Cortaderia fulvida *has been placed within arm's reach of the species* Rosa glauca*; the arch of the rose branches is echoed by the graceful curve of the feathery fronds, and the cherry-red hips of the rose appear to be strung like Christmas lights among the faded grass flowers. In summer, the pale rose flowers and soft glaucous foliage would create just as pleasing a seasonal picture.*

successful germination of most prairie plants. Then, for the first three weeks after sowing, the area must be regularly watered, just like a newly sown lawn. It is possible to begin a prairie with small transplants or plugs of rooted perennials, but for large areas seed is more economical – but it does have to be watered and mulched with clean straw if possible.

There can be as many as three hundred species of flowering perennials, annuals, bulbs and grasses in a native prairie – enough to satisfy even the most ardent gardener (a quick inventory of the perennials growing in my English garden revealed a huge number of prairie plants introduced to Britain by planthunters from the earliest days of colonialism). With such diversity it is probably wise to establish some kind of order in planting; sowing seed in areas determined by height, with tall plants like prairie docks and compassplant along the perimeters and other shorter plants like black-eyed Susan and prairie blazingstar to the front, is a good starting point. But eventually the plants will move to where they feel happiest as the prairie habitat shapes itself.

Probably the one fact most people know about prairie gardening is that burning, not mowing, is part of the management routine, and the possibility of burning down your house while doing the gardening has put some people off.

LEFT *The ruby-red autumn colours of* Acer palmatum *are enhanced by an underplanting of the groundcovering evergreen perennial* Ophiopogon planiscapus *'Nigrescens'. The drooping habit of the narrow dentate maple leaves is echoed by the downward curve of the plain narrow leaves of the monkey grass.*

But by selecting days when the wind is light and in a favourable direction and setting the fire in a circular pattern so that it burns in on itself and is naturally extinguished, goes a long way towards avoiding a general conflagration. Closely mown grass paths around and through the garden act as a natural fire break. A two- to five-year gap between burns, done in the early spring, helps the prairie to regenerate by exposing the soil so it warms earlier, and assists the seed of heat-loving prairie plants to germinate more readily. But if burning is not an option, mowing in late autumn after seed has been shed will serve the purpose as long as the debris is raked off to allow the sun to warm the soil.

Meadows can be established from scratch by sowing a grass and flower seed mix onto prepared soil, or else a lawn can be adapted by planting flower plugs directly into the turf. I did this successfully in an orchard, using oriental poppies, day lilies, columbines and cranesbill geraniums. By early autumn, the perennials were fading out of flower but the tall grass was turning to seed and the effect was quite magical in the low evening light.

Autumn is the best time to begin a meadow from scratch, and the preparation is the same as for a lawn, except that you must not add fertilizers as you do not want to encourage an overly strong growth of grass at the expense of the less robust meadow flowers. By mid spring, the grass should be long enough to give a first mowing which will allow light to reach the flowering plants. Perennial plants and bulbs can be naturalized into grass during autumn; in Chapter 2 there are details about dividing and propagating perennials, so now is

LEFT *The thistle-like seedheads of eryngium are set against a cluster of autumn colours: from the strap-like red tinted leaves of* Phormium *'Pink Panther'; from* Anomatheca laxa, *a member of the iris family with bright green, grass-like foliage, topped by sprays of coral-red flowers that turn to bead-like seed pods in the autumn; and the blue-grey* Hebe glaucophylla. *It is rare for plants not to harmonize visually if they enjoy the same growing conditions. All of these plants enjoy dry sunny conditions on free-draining soil and would be a good starting point from which to develop a rock or gravel garden bed.*

the time to experiment with plugging a few species into an area of lawn.

Autumn is when established meadows are mown; you may find that you will have to scythe down the tall grass, or use a strimmer/weed-whacker. As with a prairie it is important to rake up the debris and it is heavy work, no question about it. But the reward is a wonderful flower-filled tapestry, alive with birds and insects, and the thought that you have made a contribution, however small, to the continuity of our planet's fragile ecosystems.

INSECT FRIENDS

A grass lawn is a mono-culture, and although it may be framed by flower borders, decorated with flowering shrubs and shaded by trees it contributes little to the ecology of the garden. Many of the insects that will be attracted to the prairie or meadow plants in a natural groundcovering will be beneficial, devouring aphids, mites, beetles of all sorts, snails, slugs and so on. And if they are not present in your garden, it is possible to purchase them from specialist mail-order firms.

LEFT *The tall, clump-forming pampas grass,* Cortaderia selloana, *has to be used with care, place it where the light will catch its feathery plumes.*

RIGHT *The striped* Miscanthus sinensis *'Zebrinus' makes a good focal contrast against the less strident tones of* Stipa gigantea, *glaucous-leaved* Macleaya cordata *and the foamy seedheads of* Epilobium angustifolium.

There are two sorts of garden-friendly insect; predators, which devour their prey, and parasitoids that are species specific; a female parasitoid lays an egg or eggs on the host which is eventually consumed by the larvae hatching on or inside the host's body. The mature parasitoid then goes on to find its food in plant nectar or pollen. Lacewings, tiny, delicate emerald-green flies, are the most omnivorous of the predators, followed by ladybirds, the tiny round insects universally beloved for their endearing black-spotted, shiny red carapace. Both these predators will decimate populations of aphids, spider mites, and scale insects. Parasitoids include a number of different wasps like the trichogramma which feeds off a wide range of insect eggs, including butterfly, so if you are planting a garden to encourage these creatures, avoid trichogramma.

Members of the Compositae family are among the favourites of predaceous insects; for example, daisies, goldenrod, *Achillea* and members of the sunflower genus

Helianthus. The central boss of short stamens makes a good 'table' for the insects to feed from. Many umbellifer herbs like fennel, sweet cicely and dill are also tasty meals for some beneficial insects. Pollen- and nectar-gathering insects enjoy tubular flowers, so sages, catmint, lavenders and thymes should be grown. Cover crops (discussed in Chapter 3) will provide a rich assortment of food for these friendly bugs, in addition to fertilizing the soil when turned in during the autumn dig.

In the autumn, beneficial insects need somewhere to shelter, and garden borders where the perennials are left for the interest their seedheads and faded foliage provide, will also offer your resident bug population some protection from inclement weather. It almost goes without saying that it is inadvisable to rely too heavily on pesticides, especially if you want to encourage beneficial insects in your garden. Curiously, it appears that the predators and parasitoids are more susceptible to poison than the unwelcome insects they feed on, so it would defeat the whole exercise to spray the garden with chemicals. If you must resort to sprays try to use ones that are specific to the pest you are trying to destroy. It is even better to make regular patrols, removing any stems or foliage that are heavily infested. (And what kind of gardener would you be if you were not on the lookout for trouble!)

BUTTERFLIES

Butterflies are especially welcomed by many gardeners; I'm thrilled at the sight of the monarch butterfly migration that streams through my part of Texas each autumn, and will be planting plenty of flowers to welcome them in future years.

Butterflies go through four stages in their life cycle: egg, larva, pupa and adult, which is the point in their lives when they make their showy debut in our gardens. But it is a brief appearance, and the adult's life span can be as little as two weeks. During that time they must find a mate, lay the eggs for the next generation, all the while looking for food and avoiding becoming someone else's dinner.

And don't imagine that there will be ravening hordes of butterfly caterpillars wrecking the garden; they are highly selective about their food, unlike wide-ranging foragers such as moth caterpillars and fly and beetle larvae.

Prairie and meadow plantings will attract far more butterflies than a grass lawn or even a border of choice hybrids since many of these over-bred perennial beauties lack the nectar which is so abundant in the simple single flowers of the original species. Even if you are not creating a prairie lawn or meadow, it is worth incorporating a few of the species in formal borders and among shrubs.

Buddleja davidii is commonly called butterfly bush and, as if to disprove my statement above about hybrids, the many cultivars of this fragrant shrub will attract butterflies. The American California lilacs *(Ceanothus)* are also highly attractive to butterflies. *Viburnum* species, sumac *(Rhus*

RIGHT *At Great Dixter, Christopher Lloyd has been trying out all sorts of extreme plant combinations; the luscious mauve, pink and acid green typify the vivid colours he seems to favour, and the dull brown of the desiccated thistle is the contrast.*

autumn garden, as well as providing the necessary over-wintering shelter for beneficial insects and butterfly progeny. In the flower garden, among the butterfly perennials that would find a home in a prairie lawn are the New England aster (*Aster novae-angliae*), bergamot (*Monarda didyma*), butterfly weed (*Asclepias tuberosa*), phlox (*Phlox paniculata*), purple coneflower (*Echinacea purpurea*) and *Verbena bonariensis*.

In a prairie or meadow planting, the plants are distributed in broad drifts or colonies amongst the grasses. This suits the feeding habits of butterflies; they choose their food source by colour and a mass makes more of a show than a single plant. They also prefer to flit from one flower to another rather than lingering long over a particular blossom. And in autumn there are plenty of colourful perennials to provide fodder for migrant butterflies.

LEFT *Autumn gardens are enlivened by good foliage mixes; perennials like* Sedum *'Vera Jameson',* Euphorbia dulcis *'Chameleon',* Hieracium villosum *and the sedge,* Carex *' Frosted Curls' show what is possible.*

RIGHT *Colour and shape contrasts in the yellow-splashed foliage of* Euonymus fortunei *'Sheridan Gold' and a* Rubus *species with chocolate markings.*

typhina), dogwoods (*Cornus*) and many species of willow (*Salix*) and poplar (*Populus*) are all havens for butterfly species. Some of these plants flower in early summer, but the foliage will have something to add to the colour of the

FLAMING BORDERS

For many gardeners, flowers offer the greatest creative potential; they are the paints, textures and shapes on the horticulturist's palette, from which wonderful pictures can be composed in the beds and borders that constitute the heart of the garden.

The gardens of ancient Persia were metaphors for heaven, and in these gardens water features, fruit trees, and scented flowers were combined to create an earthly paradise. In medieval Europe, monastic cloister gardens devoted to the cultivation of herbs and vegetables served the monastic community, while the flowers grown were dedicated to altar decoration as well as being used for herbal medicines. From these symbolic and practical beginnings, early flower gardens evolved. Roses, lilies and wild flowers, collected from hedgerows, mingled with exotic shrubs and herbs from the Holy Lands, introduced by returning Crusaders, to decorate the ladies' gardens or 'flowery meads' within the castle keep. These intimate, enclosed gardens were fenced by simple

The prominence of flowers in gardens was under attack during the seventeenth and eighteenth centuries when formal parterres, endless tree-lined avenues and the Landscape Movement led by Capability Brown were imposed upon the natural landscape and the woodlands and meadows of England were sculpted into green parks. But flower gardening never really lost its place in the hearts of the common people. Grandiose schemes and the novelty of Capability Brown's 'landskip' never caught on with the more conservative land-owning gentry of England, whose gardens proved

LEFT *More of Christopher Lloyd's bold autumn planting with* Plectranthus argentatus, Anaphalis margaritacea, Aster '*Little Carlow'*, Rudbeckia fulgida *var.* deamii *and* Miscanthus sinensis *'Strictus'.*

RIGHT *At West Dean, Sussex, the autumn borders are filled with plants like* Heuchera micrantha *var.* diversifolia *'Palace Purple', nasturtiums, rudbeckias, the favourite red* Dahlia *'Bishop of Llandaff'*, Salvia confertiflora, *castor oil plant* (Ricinus communis) *and the seedheads of red orach,* Atriplex hortensis *var.* rubra.

PREVIOUS PAGE *Autumn flower borders need not be dull if much use is made of the huge Michaelmas daisy clan; at Waterperry Gardens, Oxford, the borders are filled with parti-coloured daisies, sedums, rudbeckias and goldenrod.*
INSET *Purple coneflower* (Echinacea purpurea) *is another autumn warhorse, surrounded by other seasonal stalwarts like* Persicaria amplexicaulis *'Rosea', wall valerian* (Centranthus ruber *var.* coccineus) *and* Helenium *'Kupferzwerg'.*

wooden palisades, and decorated with turf seats and shady flower-covered arbours. Such flower-filled bowers can often be seen in the background in fifteenth-century manuscript illuminations where, today, they allow us a glimpse of that romantic age. It was a simpler age for gardeners as well, as it was a time well before the introduction of a whole new world of plants which began with the discovery of South and North America and an increase in trade with Africa and the East Indies which set the course for modern flower garden design.

a refuge for the jumble of cottage garden flowers that had cheered the hearts and minds of garden-makers for centuries. These, too, were the folk who peopled the colonies, transporting their familiar flowers and gardening methods to the hostile unknown New World. But soon they were sending back wonderful new plants to Europe, thereby extending the flower palette and spurring on new developments in flowers and gardening.

For the past fifteen years at least, contemporary English gardening has been dominated by the past; by garden designers emulating the flower border plantings and cottage garden style of the Edwardian garden designer, Gertrude Jekyll. Her influential colour theory for combining flowers in long broad borders was first described in 1908 in her book *Colour Schemes for Flower Gardens*, which is still in print today. Vita Sackville-West, who created a garden during the 1930s-40s at Sissinghurst in Kent, is prominent among the world-famous English plantswomen and men whose planting schemes have been inspired by Jekyll's work.

Planting schemes designed according to these principles depend upon the dynamics of colour theory for their impact, but modern designers, perhaps sensing that it is difficult to move forward if you are always looking back, are seeking a new aesthetic, with the result that many contemporary designers and home-gardeners are approaching the making of flower gardens in a much more ecological manner; their concern is to establish a balance of nature in their flower borders rather to strive for an artistic balance of colour. They may have their differences, but one thing uniting Jekyllistes and Wild Gardeners is their mutual recognition that autumn flower gardens offer something special. For the former, the hot colours shared by autumn-flowering plants and the long growing season offered by flowering exotics from the tropics and subtropics allow them extended playtime; while the latter recognize that naturalized perennials embedded in a matrix of ornamental grasses are at their prime in autumn, as the grass seedheads make a frothy background to the composite and umbellifer perennials and annuals that populate prairie and meadow gardens.

FLOWER GARDEN PREPARATION

When planning a garden, my first manoeuvre is to chart the passage of the sun and play of shadow around the site at various times of day, and over as long a period as I can manage. Sketching in these areas on tracing paper allows me to create a layered map and to pinpoint full-sun hotspots, areas of perpetual shade, where and how far the morning sun reaches, and which areas of garden first fall into afternoon shade; essential information to help identify planting zones. Add to this any observations on areas of moist soil, wet boggy spots, or dry arid patches, frost pockets or wind catchers and the result is a pretty accurate site profile.

There are several conditions that will affect the type of flowers you will be able to grow, but many of them will do well no matter where in the garden you choose to place them, as long as the soil is well-prepared and the plants receive at least a few hours of sunshine each day. Exceptions to this are plants which specifically require full sun, full shade, dry free-draining soils, moisture-retentive soils, and combinations of these main characteristics. But one quality that effects plants, no matter what sort of condition they prefer, is the soil pH.

There are a number of soil-testing kits on the market, including gauges you poke in the ground to take a reading. Personally, I prefer the most basic technology: a test tube in which you dissolve an indicator tablet in distilled water, then add a half teaspoon of soil. Shake it well and let the soil settle until the water clears. The water will have turned to a colour which you then read against the colour chart provided in the kit, and this indicates the level of acidity or alkalinity as mentioned in the first chapter: 6.5–7 is regarded as neutral and this is what suits most plants.

I would never recommend trying to amend soils to grow acid-loving plants on alkaline soils, or vice-versa. You can make changes but over time you will find that the soil will revert, or else you will have to make the adjustments every year, and I really don't see the point in it. Keep life simple. If you really have to grow some choice lime-hating plant in your chalky garden, then do it in a container and water with rain water (the chances are that the ground water will be alkaline in a chalky area).

All flower garden preparation is done in the autumn, and most of the planting as well. Turn the soil to at least a spade depth, taking care to remove all perennial weed roots as you go. Incorporate pea gravel or turkey grit to loosen heavy soils or add rotted manure or compost to loose soils

to enhance moisture retention. Even if the garden is intended to be a dry garden, the plants will appreciate this initial improvement of the soil, particularly if you take the trouble to add the compost at a much deeper level than you might ordinarily do, as it will encourage the plants to put down deep roots in their search for moisture, and the deep-rooting will in turn sustain them through dry spells.

Hardy herbaceous perennials die down during winter; their top growth withers and melts away completely in frosty weather or else remains as a burnished skeleton continuing to contribute something to the garden picture. Meanwhile, the crown and roots remain below ground protected by the soil layer and any protective mulching you put in place during the autumn. Tender perennials are plants from exotic climates and are ones which would not survive the winter freeze outdoors; they should be lifted and brought into the greenhouse, or other frost-free place, and stored in layers of moss or peat, dry sand or grit. They can also be propagated by cuttings in late summer and then kept in the greenhouse or conservatory from autumn until the last frost of late spring.

Annuals and biennials also have much to offer the flower gardener and, since they are only passing tenants of the border, can be used to fill gaps while perennial plants are filling out. Annuals are called that because they complete their growth cycle in one year; from seed sown in autumn to flower in the following spring and early summer, setting seed again by early autumn the following year. These are hardy annuals; half-hardy annuals are generally sown in the spring

to flower through into autumn. Biennial seed is sown in the autumn of year one, establishes a root and leaf system the first year, then flowers in the second. Nursery-grown biennials are often sold in the autumn and can be planted out into their flowering positions in the garden. Winter-flowering hardy annuals like pansies, are also on the market during late summer and early autumn.

DESIGNING FOR
A FLOWER GARDEN

Following my short lecture on garden history and the type of flower gardens that are popular, the main thing to remember is that you are making a garden for your own pleasure, so anything goes if that is what makes you happy. There is enormous pleasure to be had from a carefully constructed polychromatic flower border that builds like a crescendo from the lyrical pastels of early summer to the hot

jazz flares of autumn. In my garden at Sycamore Barn, I attempted to arrange the borders by the season, so that the moisture-loving plants of early spring were against the east-facing shady side of the garden which didn't seem to dry out so much during the summer. The summer roses and their company of silver-leaved artemisias, lavender, catmint, irises and alliums went along the south-facing, sun-loving boundary, while the autumn border faced the west and the setting sun and was set against a dark yew hedge which only seemed to heighten the glow of the autumn flower colours found in Michaelmas daisies, brown-leaved grasses and sedges, and the many prairie plants I raised in homage to my American roots.

Give the plants room to breathe. By that I mean try to make the borders roomy enough to accommodate the planting without looking shoved against a fence or crammed into a corner. If you are having a lawn edged with

LEFT *Beth Chatto's gravel garden is famous for its collection of dry-loving plants, many of which are at their peak in autumn.*

RIGHT *Grass borders have much to offer the autumn gardener: in the foreground at Upper Mill Cottage the border begins with bright yellow* Hakonechloa macra *'Aureola',* blue-grey Elymus hispidus, Pennisetum orientale, P. alopecuroides, *and* Carex conica *'Hime-kan-suge'. Tall-growing grasses behind are* Miscanthus sinensis *'Flamingo',* Stipa arundinacea *(an excellent grass all year-round),* Molinia caerulea *ssp.* arundinacea, Miscanthus sinensis *'Zebrinus' with horizontal yellow bands, and* Stipa brachytricha.

perennial borders, make it proportional so that the lawn provides a setting for the plants rather than a vast green sea with a few perennials clinging onto the edges. In small back yards, you can get more planting space by laying out the beds diagonally so that the corners form deep beds around a diamond-shaped lawn. Larger gardens can have informal island beds to break up the space, with the grass areas serving as paths snaking between each area. Use lengths of laundry line or rubber hose to help define the curves of an island bed – hose has the helpful habit of curving naturally so is easier to use. Then when you have finalized the plan, grab a can of cheap spray paint and mark out the shapes to be dug.

It is often advised to arrange the plants so that the tallest are at the back of the border or in the centre of the island bed, with the size grading down to the shortest plants at the front – boring. Mix them up; this is especially true when working with autumn-flowering plants in a mixed season setting. Autumn plants, of every size, can be extremely useful in the foreground to screen the earlier flowering plants as they die down.

If you are going for the colour theme border, then you should probably make a working plan to identify exactly which plants of what colour and how many of each you will need. If you are going for a more informal plan with island beds beneath trees and/or mixed with shrubs, then you might be able to work 'freehand', assembling the perennials you wish to grow together and arranging them on the garden ground rather as Jackson Pollock dribbled paint onto a canvas – a little bit here, a little bit there – striving to achieve a balance of shape and colour or peaking interest by contrasting textures and tints.

PLANTING AND MAINTENANCE

Just as for trees and shrubs, autumn usually offers exactly the kind of planting conditions that are best for setting out perennials: mild sunny weather, perhaps with a forecast of approaching rain, and a slight breeze to cool you as you work.

Before planting out pot-grown or bare-rooted plants, or lifting transplants, water them well. Soak pots for a hour or so, put bare-rooted subjects into a bucket of water and drench nursery rows. Once you have done this, begin by putting the plants in their planting places, following your

LEFT *Flower colour changes with the seasons, and in the autumn the shades of yellow, red and blue are intense; as though they had collected all of summer's sunshine to release in a final blaze of glory. Black-eyed Susan,* Rudbeckia hirta, *and spiky* Persicaria amplexicaulis *'Rosea' are among the best for colour and contrast in autumn flower gardens.*

design or instinct; generally the plants will be container-grown and in plastic pots or polybag planters. Don't remove these until the moment of planting; they will protect the roots and prevent them from drying out as you work. Also, you may not complete all the planting in one day, so again, the pots remain as protection. If the plants are divisions or rooted cuttings that you have lifted from the border or nursery beds, wrap them in plastic or toss a dampened piece of sacking over the root ball for protection.

Once the plants are set out, try to envisage how they will look when in full flower – is there enough contrast between the foliage types to hold your interest? Will the colours complement each other? Are the contrasts you're trying to make really that successful? Most importantly, are the plants in the right place, sun lovers in the sun and so on? All your work will be in vain if you haven't suited the plant to the site.

The usual rule of thumb is to plant perennials in groups of three, five, seven (for really large borders!) and to try and create a fluid transition from one group to the next; Jekyll's plans most often show long 'drifts' running obliquely across the width of the beds. At Hidcote Manor in Gloucestershire, one of the most famous Edwardian gardens and one which had the most impact on twentieth-century English garden design, Lawrence Johnston developed a way of planting a single group of perennial plants or annuals, then a little further down the bed, planting a small cluster of the same plant, then a few feet from that planting one or two more. This gave the effect of a colony of self-sown plants and heightened the natural informality of the garden.

This is a useful way to plant grasses in a naturalistic perennial border, as the effect of natural dispersion is most pleasing and permits you to mesh the various species without it looking too 'blocky'. Another way to do this is to plant in a series of overlapping circles of various sizes; this is an especially good way to sow seed for annuals or prairie gardens.

BACK TO PLANTING SKILLS

Before planting pot-grown perennials, just as for trees and shrubs, tease out any roots that are growing around on themselves, trim away any damaged roots and remove any mossy or lichen-encrusted compost from the top layer of compost around the base of the plant. When using small divisions or rooted cuttings, I have always trimmed the roots by grasping them together just below the base of the plant and clipping away any root ends that protrude from the bottom of my clenched fist; trimming like this makes it easier to deploy the roots in the planting holes, and small feeder roots seem to develop more quickly from the clipped roots so that the plant establishes faster in its new site. Some nurseries send out bare-rooted plants; trim and tidy these if necessary (it shouldn't be, if they are from a good nursery).

Make the planting hole large enough to accommodate the root ball and deep enough so that the crown of the plant is just below the soil surface. Put the plant into the hole, fanning out the roots of bare-rooted ones and then back-fill, firming the soil around the roots with your hands as you work. Then finish off by watering well to help the soil settle around the roots of the plants. If the soil is very dry at planting time, you can fill each hole with water and let it soak away before planting. Then be sure to keep the new bed adequately watered for the first few weeks after planting. If there is rain, so much the better.

Once the perennials are in place, hardy biennials and annuals can be set out to fill gaps between the young, permanent population. Pansies and violas are especially useful since they make a cheerful show early in the year and will also help to keep down weeds. Annual plants in perennial borders look most effective in small drifts; this is a good time to use the Hidcote planting technique – it will help the annuals appear naturalized among the perennials. The final plants to add are bulbs and then any annual seeds you may be using. Try to keep bulbs in large clumps, not dotted as singles here and there; a clump makes more of an impact when in flower. Also, spring-flowering bulbs and perennials are best kept to the back of the border or behind later flowering plants, to disguise their fading flowers and foliage.

Another few words about sowing annual seed in beds and borders; in addition to using the circles method, you can draw curving seed drills in and around the perennial plants. When the seed is sown, lightly rake the soil over the drill and tamp it down with the head of the rake, then water using a fine rose on the watering can (you don't want a

RIGHT *The soft plumes of the pampas grass,* Cortaderia selloana *'Sunningdale Silver', are especially fine and make a good foil for the brighter blooms of* Sedum *'Herbstfreude' and the bright pink autumn* Cosmos, *a long-blooming annual.*

ABOVE *Plants with distinct markings set the theme for an associa-tion:* Sedum *'Stewed Rhubarb Mountain' has fine colouring, with dark red stems and mottled pink flowerheads, accenting the varie-gations of surrounding plants including* Fuchsia magellanica *var.* molinae *'Sharpitor' and variegated horseradish.*

RIGHT Persicaria amplexicaulis *'Rosea' with* Deschampsia cespi-tosa *'Goldtau' and the prairie plant,* Eupatorium purpureum *ssp.* maculatum *'Atropurpureum', make good companions, all enjoying the same growing conditions of well-drained, deep soils.*

drenching shower to wash the seed away). Unless you are especially skilled at seed sowing, it will be necessary to thin the seedlings once they have established their first true leaves. Remove the weakest of the seedlings, leaving enough space between those which remain to allow for healthy growth.

Overcrowding causes disease and weak growth as the plants compete for nutrients.

Top off the newly planted bed with a good blanket of mulch, which can be anything from clean, dry straw to well-rotted leaf compost. It will prevent winter rain from com-pacting the top layer of the soil, prevent frost penetrating the soil and heaving newly planted perennials out of the ground, and suppress weed germination in spring. It used to be the custom to use peat moss, but this is not in favour ecologically, especially when there are so many other sources of compost that are not threatened with depletion – it takes millennia for a peat bog to develop and only decades to strip it bare. Use something other than peat for mulch.

Some tall-growing perennials require staking to keep them from flopping around over their shorter neighbours, and probably the least obvious supports are twiggy branches,

placed around the clump of plants. The tops of the twigs can be snapped to bend over the crown of the plants and as the plants gain height they will gradually conceal the supports. Other methods, like bamboo canes, wire circles or crutches are hard to disguise, and least successful is a plant girdled by garden twine and tied to a stake, like some sacrificial victim. Put supports in place during autumn, after you have cut down any dead top growth. It will be impossible to do it effectively once the plant is actively growing.

During autumn, established perennial beds can be weeded and lightly dug over to loosen the topsoil. Use a three-pronged cultivator for this task, or a small border fork to work in the close quarters between established plants. This will open up the soil which may well have been compacted by rain or else baked by the sun to form a hard crust during summer. Air and moisture can then reach the roots.

A dressing of bone meal, stirred into the top soil around each plant, is beneficial. Some of the faded top growth of early midsummer-flowering plants can be cut down and certainly anything that looks unsightly should be removed. But many ornamental grasses retain their looks well into autumn. Umbelliferae and some of the Compositae will also have fine seedheads, if like the Michaelmas daisies, they are not still actively flowering. So be restrained in your autumn border cleansing; leaving seedheads is one way to have 'winter interest' in the garden.

Some less hardy perennials will be protected by their faded top-growth which serves as a loose mulch; Mexican giant hyssop (*Agastache mexicana*), Peruvian lily (*Alstroemeria aurea*), Russian sage (*Perovskia atriplicifolia*) and most of the Mediterranean herbs, are plants that appreciate the winter mantle their faded stems and leaves provide.

DEAD-HEADING

The removal of dead flowers is not strictly confined to autumn, but is something that can carry on all year, and is an activity that will, in many cases, help to prolong the attractiveness of a perennial planting. As perennials mature they begin to 'open up', becoming taller, lanker, leaner and often unkempt in overall outline. By removing faded flowers and cutting back to where healthy new shoots are emerging, you can tighten up the whole picture – as if you are pulling it back into focus – so that the bed or border continues to have eye appeal during the close of the season right up to the first frosts. When most flowers fade, they begin to produce seed; this can have a detrimental effect on foliage, which starts to look rather shabby, as the plant's functions begin to shift energy into seed production. This is particularly the case with perennials that are valued for their foliage. Not every seedhead is suited to dried flower arrangements and some are just plain unattractive, adding nothing to the garden.

Dead-heading is something to reserve for the end of the day; it is quite relaxing to wander through the garden, carefully clipping away individual faded flowers with sharp secateurs or scissors. Don't go around yanking dead blooms

LEFT *Colour contrasts in autumn flowers from the purple umbels of* Allium senescens *ssp.* montanum *var.* glaucum *and the sprays of the fine yellow-flowered* Crocosmia × crocosmiiflora *'Citronella'.*

RIGHT Crocosmia × crocosmiiflora *'Star of the East' with* Berberis thunbergii *'Harlequin'.*

from the stalk, take the time to cut back to a leaf node; buds forming at that point will be the next flush of flowers. On perennials that have sprays or clusters of flowers, cut away the entire stalk, reducing it by at least half or one-third its height to encourage more bushy growth to develop.

Some plants, like lady's mantle and hardy geraniums, are difficult to dead-head because the faded flowers are too closely engaged with the foliage. But take a look at the base of the plant and you'll see new shoots emerging, so just cut the old leaves and flower stalks back to just above the new growth. It will soon grow, and give a fresh flush of leaves and blooms for late-season glory while disguising the stubble.

Other perennials bloom in a single flush and look dishevelled the rest of season. Use long-bladed shears to remove the dead flowerheads and to clip them into shape; rue, sage, lavender and catmint fall into this category (although you can cut catmint right down to the ground and get a second blast of blue flowers for autumn).

RIGHT *One of my all-time favourite gardens was designed by Mark Brown for the Cabot Perry garden of the Museum of American Impressionism at Giverny. Taking the flora of the hills behind the village, Mark has woven an intricate carpet of grasses, herbs and flowering shrubs for a garden on a south-facing site that is fairly dry and certainly sun-baked. Although lovely all year long, it really reaches its finest moment in the autumn, when the soft biscuit tints of the many grasses such as* Stipa gigantea, Sesleria caerulea *and* Brachypodium sylvaticum *are dotted with sweeps of blue flower from sage,* Perovskia, Eryngium, *catmint, clary sage, hyssop and* Catananche. *This exquisite garden perfectly captures the essence of the 'Impressionist' garden, painted with the colours of nature as nature herself might have mixed them.*

ABOVE *Grasses are the ultimate autumn border plant, making perfect 'blenders' for flowers and other foliage plants; cultivars of maiden grass,* Miscanthus sinensis, *are among the best, as this border in another Mark Brown-designed garden shows. From the front, there is M. s. 'Nippon', M. s. 'Flamingo', a stand of* Coreopsis tripteris *and the tall-growing species itself,* M. sinensis.

RIGHT *The feathery pink-tinted plumes of* Stipa arundinacea *are among the most tactile of the grass flowers and this particular stipa is hard to beat. It makes a beautiful mound of soft greeny-gold that blends well with plants like* Yucca flaccida *'Golden Sword' and yellow-leaved shrubby honeysuckle,* Lonicera nitida *'Baggesen's Gold'.*

Many tall-growing, leggy perennials can be 'stunted' to prevent them becoming gangling and over-bearingly awkward; in early summer, after they have made a growth of about 60cm (2ft), shear them back by one-third or more if you want to considerably reduce their stature. It will make the plant stouter, as well as shorter as it regrows, and delay its flowering period.

PROPAGATION – DIVISION

There are several methods of propagation for perennial plants, but the easiest is division, and with few exceptions – namely grasses and silver-leaved plants – autumn is the best time of year for this task.

Perennials grow from the centre, putting on new growth around the outside edge of the clump. As the clump matures, the centre can die out or become weaker, producing less foliage and fewer flowers. Consequently, most perennials grown in conventional beds and borders benefit from being lifted and divided every three to five years.

Water the plant you are going to divide several hours before you start, then use a spade to dig around the periphery of the plant to cut through the roots, then lever it out of the soil with a fork. If the plant is a clump-forming perennial, and the clump is dinner-plate sized or greater, jam two garden forks back to back into the centre of the clump and then pull them apart; this should split the root ball. These smaller clumps can be further divided by pulling them apart by hand into smaller planting-sized pieces, or else by teasing them apart with a hand fork. The main thing is to aim for several growing points on each clump and enough roots to support new growth. Tuberous-rooted perennials or rhizomatous plants can be cut up with a sharp knife; just be sure that there is a healthy growing point on each piece and a few root nodes.

Many bulbous plants, like crocosmia, alliums and so on, produce offsets, which are small bulbs that form around or at the base of the parent bulb. These tiny bulbils can be rubbed off, often with a tiny root attached, and planted on; and will usually produce flowering plants in two years.

to divide it into separate plants which should be potted up and grown on for at least one year before planting out. This method also works with lilies that form small bulbils along the stem, such as tiger lilies (*Lilium lancifolium*).

ROOT CUTTINGS

Oriental poppies (*Papaver orientale*) are among the plants that can be increased by root cuttings; that is why if you ever try to transplant an oriental poppy you will never be able to move it entirely, any piece of root left behind will make a new plant. Others like this are bear's breeches (*Acanthus mollis*), bleeding heart (*Dicentra spectabilis*) and *Ligularia*; generally any plants with stringy roots can be raised using this method.

Lift a clump of the parent plant, remove a well-rooted section and replant the parent. Select lengths of root that are

LEFT *Designer Mark Brown's* Miscanthus *garden shows the tall-growing ornamental grasses to best effect across the broad expanse of an unmown meadow.*

RIGHT *Constance Kargére has introduced some stunning combinations for year-long interest in the double borders that frame the entrance to her family home, Bois des Moutiers. Gertrude Jekyll apparently provided plans for entirely impractical annual borders for the Lutyen's designed house. Constance has the same fine eye for colour as Jekyll, but a more practical sense of planting using* Berberis thunbergii *'Rose Glow' with a claret-red dahlia.*

STEM CUTTINGS

Some plants, like species of *Sedum*, produce stubby little shoots in their leaf axils – the point where the leaf attaches to the stem. These infant plants can be encouraged to root by cutting the entire stem, trimming off the flowerhead and laying the stem in a box of sandy compost. Cover the stem with a layer of moist compost and put in coldframe or sheltered spot. The plantlets will form roots; then cut the stem at least 6mm (¹/4in) in diameter and cut them into pieces between 5–7.5cm (2–3in) long. Dunk the pieces in a fungicide solution and then lay the pieces of root in a box of moist, sandy compost. Cover lightly with more compost and water well before placing in a coldframe or greenhouse. By the following spring, new plants will have formed and each can be potted up separately.

STRATIFICATION

Establishing prairie or meadow gardens can take many more plants than we would wish to purchase, which is a good reason to grow your own from seed. Many of the perennial plants we use for these gardens require a period of exposure to cold moist conditions before they will successfully germinate in the spring. Columbines (*Aquilegia* ssp.), monkshood (*Aconitum* ssp.) and the many coneflowers, rudbeckias and other prairie natives respond well to this treatment.

Seed can be sown in early autumn in small pots, seed trays or flats, or in specially prepared seedbeds outdoors, in a mix of 50-50 coarse sand and fibrous potting mix. Label the pots and trays and place them in an open coldframe in a sheltered, preferably north-facing, spot in the garden. Keep moist; if the compost dries out, water lightly. The seed will not germinate all at once; some may take up to a year to shoot, while others will leap into life. As and when the seed sprouts, move the container into a spot where they will receive indirect light. Setting the containers on gravel or coarse grit will help to deter slugs and snails, or use your usual slug bait to protect the young seedlings.

As the seedlings fill out, prick them out into individual containers or nursery rows covered with a cloche or floating fabric mulch until they are settled in. Then let the young plants develop until autumn the following year when they can be planted out.

If you need to sow seed earlier, or if your climate is too mild to provide the winter chill needed, sow the seed in small pots and place in the refrigerator for at least six weeks.

NATURALIZING GRASSES

In the first chapter I talked about prairie lawns and meadows as alternatives to conventional grass lawns, and at the start of this chapter about the move towards more naturalistic perennial borders, modelled on the way plants form communities in the wild. To my eye, these plantings offer the greatest autumn interest and, in fact, make winter gardening something to seriously consider. I have never really believed in 'Winter Gardens', preferring to stay indoors when it is cold and anticipate the arrival of the first spring bulbs. My scepticism was reinforced when Sally sent me a photo of her winter garden in Boston – everything was hidden by a deep blanket of snow and it could have been shrubs or dustbins beneath the lumpen white shapes that dotted her small garden.

Contemplating a matrix of fine-leaved grasses on a snowy day is what changed my mind: the beauty of grasses like cultivars of the maiden grass, *Miscanthus sinensis* 'Gracillimus', *M.s.* 'Morning Light', *M.s.* 'Silberspinne' or *M.s.* 'Undine'; or species of stipa, like *Stipa tenuissima* or *S. arundinacea*, and switch grass, *Panicum virgatum*. Snow does not seem to build up on their narrow leaves, and in the case of *Miscanthus* especially the flower stems remain fairly stiff and do not double over under frost or snow. Instead they kept their form pretty well, with their skeleton stems held high above the drifting snow and wispy foliage rustling in the winter chill. Other cold-weather structure grasses are Ravenna grass (*Saccharum ravennae*) and some of the everblues (they appear more blue than green!) and bronzes,

like blue oat grass (*Helictotrichon sempervirens*) or the eye-catching bronze-leaf sedge, *Carex buchananii*.

These are clump-forming grasses, and most of them are very tall indeed – Ravenna grass is like a refined pampas grass, and can reach up to 3.5m (12ft) in height, while the sedge makes bristly clumps about 60cm (2ft) tall. Generally, I would say that to ensure they have enough space to grow elegantly they should be planted at least as far apart as they are tall; in a mixed group be guided by the tallest plant. Use the very tallest grasses as signature plants, but treat other sizes as you would other flowering perennials, creating drifts from

ABOVE *Zinnias are particularly fine annual flowers that are at their best from late summer to first frost.*

to plant in the spring. However, I have successfully planted in autumn which is useful if you're incorporating herbaceous perennials in the scheme. It is an unbroken rule that all division and transplanting be done in spring when the grasses are again growing strongly.

Plant grasses exactly as you would any other perennial. Add some bone meal to the back-fill to give the grass something extra to work with as it settles in. Once the plants are established, there is no need to feed. But pay attention to watering and do it regularly during the first year as new roots are put out. But, as with feeding, once the plants are established, most of them will be fairly drought tolerant.

Grooming grasses is important to help maintain vigour as well as appearances and should be done in late winter or early spring. *Miscanthus* and other grasses that die back should be cut down to within 15cm (6in) of the ground. Others that are evergreen or semi-evergreen can be 'combed' with a rake to remove dead foliage and flower stems.

Perennials that carry their flowers on long stems, or ones which have trailing, scrambling stems, work best with grasses; many of the best are autumn-flowering, daisy-type plants from the Compositae family. The Michaelmas daisies offer a huge range of colour and flower size from which to choose and there are several sorts of coneflower (*Echinacea*), including the white-petalled *E. purpurea* 'White Swan'. The goldenrods, *Solidago*, have plenty of interesting yellow-flowered family members of varying heights – from 30cm to 1.5m (1 to 5ft) – and habits – from the rigidly upright *S. rigida*, which makes erect stems up to 1.5m (5ft) tall topped with

the smallest, and significant groups or clusters from medium-sized sorts. Mingle herbaceous perennials among the grass clumps; purple coneflower among the purple-tinted caterpillar-like plumes of fountain grass (*Pennisetum alopecuroides*), or yellow-flowered black-eyed Susan (*Rudbeckia hirta*) among the brassy green of *Stipa arundinacea*.

Most grasses will be container-grown so they can be planted at any time of year, although the general practice is

fluffy yellow pompons, to *S. rugosa*, that has a wide spread of arching stems bearing clusters of bright yellow flowers along their tips.

Sedums flower in autumn and are valuable for their ruddy tints and unusual foliage colours, ranging from the red of *Sedum telephium* 'Matrona' to the variegated green and white *S.* 'Gooseberry Fool'. Japanese anemones, or windflowers, have a stalky upright habit that mingles well with clumpforming grasses. Phlox and *Verbena bonariensis* are other good upright perennials to use among grasses.

Foliage contrasts that work well with grasses can be found among members of the Umbelliferae family. The erect stems and saucer-shaped flowerheads among this group of plants also work well with clumping grasses. Fennel, sweet cicely, dill, Queen Anne's lace, wild and cultivated carrot, angelica and even parsnips are all part of this

LEFT *In England, Beth Chatto has, through the example of her show gardens in Essex and her many fine books, encouraged gardeners to suit the plant to the site. While it may be possible to amend the soil, making it more acid or alkaline to suit whatever it is you want to grow, the amendment will not endure and will have to be repeated periodically to keep the plants healthy. It makes more sense to work with what you have. Observe the conditions of your soil, the amount of light or shade the planting zone receives and the moisture levels, and plant accordingly. In dry shade, few things do better than groundcovers like epimediums and periwinkles; they also provide an excellent background to the autumn-flowering colchicums, disguising the colchicums' faded foliage after flowering.*

family and have the characteristic ferny foliage and lacy white flower clusters. But some of the umbellifers have attractive purple foliage, like the biennial herb *Angelica gigas*, or the delicate dove-grey form of cow parsley, *Anthriscus sylvestris* 'Ravenswing'.

Eryngiums are thistle-like umbellifers and the leathery leaved sea holly, *Eryngium maritimum*, has a good dense grey colour. Its relative, *E. bourgatii* is tinged with blue, while *E.* × *zabelii* has the bluest flowers and bracts of all.

One of the chief delights of having grasses in the garden is for the beauty of their seedheads. However, with some species the seed can all too readily self-sow, as I found with *Deschampsia cespitosa*. This is one of the loveliest grasses for autumn and winter interest, with dark green glossy foliage topped by a cloud of flower panicles that fade to soft golden brown in winter. But it seeds in a frenzy and soon a seething crowd of juvenile plants was inching its way throughout the border. Of course, it is easy to weed them out (and then pot them up to pass along to other gardeners, with a warning about its invasive nature, of course), and this is probably the best way to deal with free self-sowers. Rather than try to decapitate the plants and loose their autumn glory in the process, stay on top of the weeding to keep the population in check.

AUTUMN BULBS

In her 1936 book, *Adventures with Hardy Bulbs*, the American garden writer Louise Beebe Wilder, gave a good definition of what it means to naturalize bulbs:

ABOVE *Colchicums grown with petunias is another of Christopher Lloyd's bright ideas – very bright in fact. These charming autumn bulbs are rarely associated with other flowers, doing their time in horticultural purdah wherever their ungainly foliage won't be too obvious.*

RIGHT *Cyclamen, however, enjoy a devoted following and are encouraged to naturalize where they will.*

'In its narrow sense, to naturalize bulbs means merely to plant them in an informal and unstudied manner in contra-distinction to their use in formal beds; but in the broader and more accepted sense, it means to broadcast them on a generous scale in woods, in meadows… on rough banks or about the outskirts of the garden, to suggest, as best we may, nature's handicraft, not man's.'

The most effective way to give a naturalized appearance is to plant bulbs in masses or in clusters of one variety so that it seems as if a self-sown or mature group has spread under its own steam over the years. Although bulbs for naturalizing are fairly rugged characters, they do best where competition is not too strong, so avoid planting at the base of shallow-rooting trees or shrubs, or in areas where there is thick groundcover or sturdy turf. In lawns and grassy meadows select areas where the groundcover is sparse or at least not strongly growing. Peel back flaps of turf, lightly digging over the exposed soil and then scatter a handful of bulbs across the surface. Replace the turf flap and tamp it down. The bulbs will come through the grass easily.

The autumn crocus is not really a crocus and is properly known as *Colchicum*. Colchicums are especially good at naturalizing and will rapidly form a substantial colony; plant them along a woodland edge or amidst the perimeter plants of naturalized perennial beds so that their dishevelled appearance during spring and summer is camouflaged. The common name for these bulbs is naked ladies, because the autumn flower appears without foliage; this appears – untidily – in the spring and dies away during summer.

Crocus speciosus is a true crocus that flowers in autumn. It gradually makes a colony of millions of tiny bulbs that produce delicate violet-blue flowers quite early in the autumn, amid a thicket of narrow green leaves. These little flowers look marvellous in orchards where the grass grows weakly in the shade of the fruit trees.

Cyclamen have always held a special appeal for me; their tiny little winged flowers pushing proudly up through a blanket of autumn leaves is enormously encouraging. The foliage too is extremely attractive, and the ivy-leaved cyclamen, *Cyclamen hederifolium*, has wonderful foliage marked with silvery veins. The larger the corm the bigger the leaves. They do best in light shade and loose sandy soil among shrubs, or with other small stature perennials. The corms have little hairy roots protruding around their girth and the young leaves will be tightly curled at the crown. Plant them so that the crown is just below the surface of the soil in small colonies and about 10–15cm (4–6in) apart. Cyclamen self-sow and you can collect the seedlings to transplant and enlarge the colonies, or you can collect the little round seed-pods. Sow the seeds in trays of sandy compost after soaking them first to aid germination.

Among the countless spring- and summer-flowering bulbs, the alliums offer the best hope for the autumn garden by virtue of their uncommonly attractive seedheads. *Allium cristophii* is deservedly popular for the starry little silvery blue flowers that form a large cluster atop the rigid stalk. These dry perfectly well *in situ* and look terrific among autumn grasses. *A. schubertii* needs a little protection to survive a mild winter, but the flowerhead is at least 45cm (18in) across and like *A. cristophii*, dries into an eye-catching ball of spiky stars.

Curiosities like these combined with the flower-garden stalwarts are what make autumn gardens lively and interesting. They pique our interest and make the hard work of autumn garden chores worthwhile.

HARVESTING
THE GARDEN

While I admit to a childlike enthusiasm for misty days and kicking up piles of autumn leaves just to hear their dry rustle, it is the mellow fruitfulness of the season that really gets me worked up. All those ripening pumpkins, ears of late sweetcorn as succulent as chunks of honeycomb, beets, chard, crisp romaine, tangy endive and crunchy 'Gravenstein' apples plucked from the bough, are enough to make one forget the fraught moments of drought, pests and disease that so often accompany the summer gestation of all this autumn bounty. Good thing too, or we'd never know the thrill of a homegrown tomato, or the clean bite of a freshly harvested onion. Riches indeed.

As a place to begin learning about gardening, you could hardly do better than to begin by sowing a row or two of annual vegetables, add a couple of perennials like rhubarb or artichokes, a gooseberry shrub and an apple tree and you will have experience of each major garden plant group. And then you get to eat the results! Furthermore, all the important

of muck or compost and fertilizer. This is traditionally how vegetable gardens are managed and how I began my veg growing, until I discovered 'raised beds'. Already popular in the USA and Europe, in Britain in the early 1980s raised beds were a novel approach – and caused a few raised eyebrows down at the allotments where I exercised my new skills. In 1988, I wrote of the wonders of raised beds in *The Art of the Kitchen Garden*. This method allows you to fertilize, cultivate, water and generally focus your energy on only those pieces of ground that are used for growing. Pathways separate the beds, and these are left untilled, but not exactly unloved since they must be kept as weed free as possible.

To construct raised beds, mark out the areas to be dug no more than 1.2m (4ft) wide, so that the middle of each bed can be reached from the side, and as long as you want. Paths between the beds can be 45–60cm (1¹/₂–2ft) wide and can be paved, gravelled, grassed (which must be mown

LEFT *Bright red terracotta rhubarb forcers and late sunflowers decorate a functional space.*

RIGHT *Apple cordons trained along a wire fence divide this traditional vegetable garden.*

PREVIOUS PAGE *Even brussels sprouts are attractive additions to the garden if you grow an ornamental variety like 'Rubine' with purple-tinted foliage.*

INSET *Highly visible in the autumn kitchen garden, the ornamental gourd 'Lemon Cucumber' adds bright spots of colour.*

garden tasks assigned to autumn also happen in the kitchen garden: digging, sowing, planting, cutting back, cleaning up, composting – what have I left out?

The basics of digging are described in the Introduction; in the kitchen garden the technique is no different if you follow what I have always called 'flat earth' methods, when the vegetable garden ground is tilled in its entirety, like a micro-version of a farm field, turning in a blanket covering

regularly) or mulched with woodchip, straw or other inert material. Edge the beds if you like or simply bank and firm. The beds are 'raised' by the extra deep layer of well-rotted manure and compost that is added to the bottom of the trench. This technique does require copious amounts of the best muck you can get.

As always when digging, work methodically, from one end of the bed to the other. The first trench of soil you remove should be dumped at the end of the bed where you will dig the final trench, and used to back-fill. The finishing touch is to tidy round the edges of each bed, making a narrow gutter between the path and the bed and firming the gently sloping raised sides.

Once the beds are established, the compost is added to the top layer and lightly forked in. Because the beds are never walked on the soil is not compacted and so it is better aerated, and routine digging is unnecessary. The openness of the soil means that it warms earlier in the year, so crops can be sown sooner, and that the fertility is high, so they can also be grown closer together. In the spring, rake the surface to a fine tilth and get sowing.

COVER CROPPING

In the autumn, as a bed is cleared of its crop you can make a late-season sowing of an over-wintering crop or dress it with a layer of rotted manure or compost. This is also mutually beneficial to both gardeners and earthworms. These creatures will thank you for the food source by taking the manure down into the soil, an action which is really

good for improving heavy soils. Alternatively, sow a 'green manure', a leafy, quick-growing crop.

It is important to not leave soil bare between crops; rain can wash away valuable nutrients, erode the beds and create a hard compacted surface. A green manure crop however, takes the nutrients into its developing structure of leaves, roots and stems to later release the goodness back into the soil when the crop is dug into the beds and then decomposes. The growing crop protects the soil surface and when dug in, becomes a valuable soil conditioner. There are green manures to suit most garden needs: some are deep-rooting and draw nutrients from the lower soil levels that are released

ABOVE *Thistle flowerheads are at their best in autumn and are especially valued by flower arrangers. This is* Carlina acaulis *bronze form.*

as the crop's foliage decomposes, others draw atmospheric nitrogen to their roots where bacteria convert it to a form that will supplement present levels of soil nitrogen.

Over-wintering green manures that protect the soil and prevent the leaching out of nitrogen are sown in autumn; among the best for this purpose are winter tares and field beans (*Vicia sativa* and *V. faba*), crimson clover (*Trifolium incarnatum*) and grazing rye (*Secale cereale*); in the spring, to condition soil before sowing late autumn and winter crops, use *Phacelia tanacetifolia*, the herb fenugreek (*Trigonella foenum-graecum*) or buckwheat (*Fagopyrum esculentum*). The buckwheat and the phacelia are quite pretty, with white and blue flowers respectively, and they are also attractive to bees. Clover cover crops are natural habitats for ladybirds; they feed on the aphids that are attracted to the clover and then the ready food source that is available encourages the ladybirds to mate and lay eggs. The emerging larvae then shelter in the clover foliage.

With their geometric form and system of pathways, raised-bed gardening is akin to the highly desirable historic 'potager' garden, where flowers, fruit and vegetables are grown together in an edible landscape design. Integral to this idea is the concept of companion planting, a growing partnership where flowers, vegetables and fruit are planted together to their mutual benefit, either as a natural means of pest control (garlic with roses to keep aphids away), or to promote healthier growth (datura with pumpkins). But the main attribute of companion planting is as a benign method of pest control. This was recognized centuries ago, when households relied on 'strewing herbs' to keep vermin levels down; lavender, sweet sedge, sage, tansy and hyssop are just a few of the plants whose branches and leaves were scattered on the floor to deter fleas, lice and so on. In French, the word *garde-robe* was the common name of southernwood, *Artemisia abrotanum;* its pungent foliage was used to keep moths out of linen cupboards. Translate this to the kitchen garden and use fragrant herbs to protect vegetables.

One of the most popular and widely used floral pesticides is the french marigold (*Tagetes*), along with other potent-smelling plants it can be used to edge or partner vegetables, disguising their scent, while the marigold's roots secrete a chemical that soil nematodes find off-putting. Insects find their food source by scent and shape; one of the cleanest rows of carrots I ever grew was between rows of onions interspersed with another marigold, *Calendula officinalis*. I like to think that the carrot fly couldn't smell its favourite food, but maybe it just couldn't see it! It has been discovered that the weed-free plot, with widely spaced neat rows stands a greater chance of pest infestation by insects that rely on sight to find their food source: a tidy row of cabbages neatly outlined against an immaculately hoed soil stands out like a sore thumb to any passing aphids and whitefly. Also, many beneficial insects will be attracted by the pollen or nectar flower companions can offer: for example, hoverflies like to sip nectar, and hoverfly larvae feed on aphids. So, intercropping with companionable plants and the close row planting that raised beds support is a good thing on many levels.

INTERCROPPING

Travel is a garden-lover's best teacher; by exploring other people's gardens we can learn new techniques, discover new plants and generally broaden our horticultural horizons, a sort of intellectual intercropping, sowing the seeds of some new idea beneath the protective mantel of proven practice. For example, in England raised beds are good because in a wet climate, they drain more freely; but a visit to Bahrain showed me how to deal with the hot dry conditions I will now contend with in Texas. Instead of raising the beds I will sink them to form water-retentive reservoirs that can be periodically flooded beneath a protective straw mulch.

Rather less fancifully, intercropping means making the most of the vegetable garden space by sowing a fast growing crop between or among a slower, longer-standing crop. In Italy, in a typical rural *horto* of the sort that seems to occupy any space of open ground ('if it's empty, plant it' is the motto there), I first saw intercropping in practice. In a small household garden, the grape vines had been trained into a sort of low, sheltering arbour, tomato vines climbed canes fixed between each vine, and cabbages grew at their feet, shading the roots of the taller plants. The garden was pretty to look at, simple in its application, and economic in it uses.

Leaf crops like lettuce and spinach can be succession-sown among onions, garlic, leeks, beans, beets, turnips and other crops that take some time to reach maturity. Brassica crops do well when interplanted with dill and fennel, and I especially like the autumn-harvest look of pumpkins and squash crops growing between rows of sweetcorn. This takes up a lot of space, and if you have it, try it. The pumpkins do well with the regular watering sweetcorn receives.

RIGHT *Elder is a common hedgerow shrub or small tree, and the shadowy tint of* Sambucus nigra *'Guincho Purple' is especially seductive. Elderberries make a tangy jelly and can be part of the blend for hedgerow wine, made only in the autumn.*

A WORD ABOUT EARTHWORMS

Earlier I described the symbiotic relationship between earthworms and gardeners; like digging, you can't garden without them. In fact, they are nature's diggers. I read some amazing statistics to the effect that each earthworm turns a ton of soil a day and that without their recycling action of dragging vegetable (and other) waste into the soil to aid decomposition, our world would be waist high in unsavoury detritus in the time it takes to say 'knife'. So, let's hear it for earthworms. (I must own up that even though it gives me a rush to see a healthy population churning away in my compost heaps, I still find it's kind of creepy to touch them!)

Never mind, this autumn I built a wormery. With the restricted space of my new Texas garden, there is not enough room for the usual compost heap. Instead, a plastic waste bin/garbage can has been punctured all round by drilling holes in the sides and had large drainage holes cut in the bottom, and has been installed in a shady corner. Red wrigglers, the compost worms *par excellence*, can be bought, although they may already live in the garden and could emigrate. About 450g (1lb) of worms per bin is sufficient.

Just like a compost heap, a wormery is filled in layers, alternating vegetable kitchen waste, annual weeds, other

LEFT & RIGHT *Trees laden with ripening apples and pears are a heart-warming sight and with their mouth-watering colours make an attractive inclusion in the mixed border, although they are more often confined to orchards.*

MEANWHILE, BACK IN THE POTAGER...

In her ground-breaking book (an unavoidable pun, I'm afraid), *Creative Vegetable Gardening*, Joy Larkcom clearly and vividly sets out everything you could possibly need to know about how to make a potager. She is particularly lyrical on ornamental vegetables – the ones that are showy enough to make it into the flower garden – and several of these are especially useful to carry interest through autumn and well into winter throughout the garden. Foremost among these must be ruby-stemmed Swiss chard. Few vegetable plants are easier to grow from seed and a row sown several weeks before the last frost will give you clusters of ruby-stemmed plants to spice up foliage groups in beds and borders or to accent the potager. It doesn't respond too well to transplanting, so raise plants in small pots in a cold frame to plant out with as little root disturbance as possible.

Ornamental cabbages are familiar stock in garden centres among trays of winter pansies and other seasonal flowering plants. And rightly so, since the foliage takes some beating for colour – from rich vinous purple to pure white, with all shades of red and glaucous blue-green in between. The leaves are often very finely cut, like a neck ruff of Flanders lace in a painting by Van Dyck, or broad and spreading with heavily frilled edges. I have often seen these planted out in evenly spaced rows of bedding – a not very inspired use of something better treated as an eccentric and planted in loose groupings amongst other strongly coloured plants. Red-leaved mustard greens and giant curled mustard

reasonably soft garden waste and so on, with layers of worm bedding which can be anything: garden soil, shredded newspaper, straw or sawdust litter, or autumn leaves (run the mower over the leaf heap a few times to shred it coarsely). The bedding has to be evenly moist before adding it in a 50-50 ratio to the waste. I exclude animal-derived waste of any kind and will only add grass mowings a little at a time. I'm eagerly anticipating my first harvest of wormcast compost, which is guaranteed to be the best soil conditioner going.

greens are ornamental in the same way and ideal for warmer climates where the cabbage might struggle.

Amaranthus is another annual flower or vegetable, depending on how you care to use it: the foliage of leafy Chinese amaranth has purple markings suffusing the centre of each leaf, while 'Red Stripe' has, as you might imagine, red along the central vein. Sow *Amaranthus* in bold patches and harvest it to eat like spinach. Grain amaranth, on the other hand, has tassel-like flower plumes that come in shades of bright yellow, dusky bronze, green and dark mahogany red. The renowned Dutch plantsman, Piet Oudolf, grows a 1.5m (5ft) tall bronze form of amaranth as an ornamental plant in perennial borders.

Even chilli peppers offer some fiery autumn colours, as well as flavours, of course. In southwestern US gardens the tiny little pecquin pepper can be seen casting its incendiary ruby red beads over rocks and through grasses. I've been told that they register more than 30,000 Scovilles (the unit of measurement for chilli heat) – increasing my admiration for the Mexican gardeners I know who munch them by the handful with their lunchtime tortillas.

LEFT *Remember the glory of glossy red currant beads – this is 'Red Lake' – they can add a sassy glimmer to shrubberies or sharp tang to fruit glazes on pies or in preserves.*

RIGHT *Hedges will often be overrun by blackberries, but in the kitchen gardens their snaking rampant canes should be controlled by pruning and training against wire supports.*

Rocambole or top-set garlic, leeks, onions and other 'vegetable' alliums have a delightful flowering habit, making flower buds on the tips of the leaves, each one wearing a pointy little cap which is doffed as the flower bursts open. Artichokes and cardoons have some of the finest 'architectural' foliage in the plant kingdom. They make stately plants up to 1.5m (5ft) tall, with broad, grey felted leaves that are divided like an acanthus leaf (also a favourite ornamental for the autumn garden). Red-leafed orach is an old

LEFT *Figs need a long hot summer to ripen, but these trees are worth growing for the shade cast by their distinctive leaves with a fragrance redolent of warm Mediterranean evenings.*

RIGHT *The grape vine* Vitis 'Brant' *produces juicy purple berries, highlighted by the rich autumn colour of the foliage.*

standby with claret-coloured leaves; it and bronze fennel will seed around lasciviously, and once they take on height are hard to pull out. So think of your back muscles and weed out ill-placed plants before they take you out! Shiso, or perilla, is another dark-leafed vegetable that is often used as a bedding plant to provide a background to showy annuals. One of the most startling bedding displays I ever saw incorporated cardoons, ruby chard, brown and parrot-green grain amaranths and red-leafed sweetcorn. It was outlandish but succeeded because it was done with such flare and conviction. Look through a good vegetable seed catalogue and you'll discover a world of decorative edibles from which to create your own unique autumn vegetable show.

AUTUMN FARE

One of the most vivid portraits of the art and craft of vegetable gardening was painted by the American comic genius, S.J. Perelman, in his series of articles for the *New Yorker*, titled 'Acres and Pains'. Anyone who has ever bought a 'place in the country' or entertained visions of homegrown produce swelling the larder, and waistline, should read these achingly funny essays, describing Perelman's experiences as a landowner in rural Bucks County, Pennsylvania during the 1940s. Let me share with you his take on the summer harvest, arrived at only after much expense, 'untold agonies' and encounters with man-eating snails:

'By the end of August the residue left by the rabbits and woodchucks is ready for harvest. It is always the same – tomatoes and squash. [They] never fail to reach maturity… Soon the most casual acquaintances start dropping in with creaking baskets and hypocritical smiles, attempting to fob off their excess tomatoes and squash. The more desperate even abandon tiny bundles on our doorstep like infants at the House of the Good Shepherd. The kitchen becomes an inferno, and the wife a frenzied sorceress stirring caldrons of pink slush… The only solution is to plow everything under and live on pie.'

As someone who has toiled more hours than she might wish over steaming pink slush and had tons of squash and tomatoes rejected at the orphanage door, I can tell you in all honesty that the only solution is to go cold turkey and toss tempting seed catalogues into the bin the moment they arrive, or resolve to grow less. Much less. Or sow smaller quantities of more varieties – do you really need such a long row of squash plants? Also, with some things it seems that no matter how carefully you organize the sowing calendar, religiously making successional sowings of lettuce or spinach at biweekly interludes or longer, chances are they will all be ready at once.

However, we know that our resolve will weaken, so let's make the harvest a good one by taking care to pick when the crops are at their prime, since fruit and vegetables in good condition are the best to use for preserving and freezing – and eating.

Water is crucial to the successful growth of crops, so water well and regularly, and in the morning if you use a sprinkler or overhead watering system as overnight moisture can encourage mildew and other blights. A soak or drip hose laid along the raised beds is a good way to ensure adequate, economical watering. The water goes directly where it is needed and there is considerably less water loss through evaporation. The bulb-forming vegetables, from garlic to turnips, will grow more quickly and be more succulent if watered well; sweetcorn, courgette/zucchini, aubergine/eggplant, pumpkins and melons also require lots of water throughout their life cycle. Conversely, too much water after fruit sets causes grapes and tomatoes to crack and strawberries to be squishy and flavourless.

As they begin to mature, check regularly that potato tubers and carrot tops are adequately covered by soil, and if necessary draw up extra soil along the rows since exposure to sunlight causes the vegetables to turn green and green potatoes must not be eaten. When onions, shallots, garlic and potatoes are ready to harvest, do not water for a week and then lift on a warm sunny morning; gather the potatoes immediately the soil is dry and doesn't cling to the tubers. Turn onions up and leave on the garden so that the sun can dry the roots and base of each bulb before gathering in.

Peas, beans, summer squash (courgette/zucchini) and pickling cucumbers will continue to flower and be productive if regularly picked over, otherwise the plant starts seed making and production shuts down. Also, most vegetables taste better when harvested young; beets the size of golf-balls, carrots only as big as a finger, courgettes the moment the flower drops off (or pick the flower to eat deep-fried in light tempura batter) and glossy green snow peas that are little-finger size. Gather bean crops before the pod goes 'bumpy', but leave soup beans to mature on the vine.

Sweetcorn fanatics insist that the best time to harvest is the when the water is boiling – so that the fresh ears can be dropped instantly into the cooking pot. This not so urgent now that there are hybrids that keep their sugar longer before turning to starch, but generally the ear is ripe when the tassels turn brown and the sap from a punctured kernel runs milky white rather than clear.

Apples, tomatoes, strawberries, raspberries, plums, okra (lady's finger) and melons are ripe when they literally fall into your hand when touched; they should not have to be cut or pulled. Sweet peppers, brussels sprouts and rhubarb should be gently twisted to separate them from the plant.

HARVEST FAIR

The harvest festivals that have been celebrated since the dawn of settled agrarian civilisations, acknowledged the handing over of power from Flora the goddess of spring and summer flowers to Ceres and Pomona, the goddesses of agriculture and fruitfulness. In rural England, before the Industrial Revolution and the mechanization of farming, it was the custom at harvest to dress the final wheatsheaf cut and to braid it and ornament it as a 'kirn baby' or 'corn dolly', representing the spirit that was thought to dwell in each ear of wheat. And because it was such bad luck to be the person who made the final cut, and supposedly kill the last of summer's bounty, the reapers would take it in turn to swing their scythes as they worked the field, mowing down the standing grain together, so that no single person would be cursed with bad luck. Today, village harvest festivals are usually centred on floral displays in the parish church, and it is a great time to stock up on home-made jams and fruit

RIGHT *A shaded walk planted with hazelnuts is a marvellous sight. In spring, soft green tassels hang down from the shadowy branches and on breezy days you can watch the pollen float from tree to tree, ensuring that autumn's crop of cobs and filberts.*

preserves, cakes and pies, made by the villagers and sold at the fêtes and bazaars which are part of harvest time.

In Britain, corn dollies are made from clean straw that is plaited into intricate patterns, with the grain-bearing ears of wheat topping off the doll like a golden crown. I recall the corn dollies from my Illinois childhood which were made from the broad flat leaves left after shucking the ears of corn bought by the bushel-full from roadside stands. And then we made corncob pipes for bubble-blowing contests using soapy water – that weren't particularly successful.

But there are other festivals marking the passage of autumn, and Michaelmas, or St. Michael's Day is the next important one to be celebrated. An antique poem describing the calendar in terms of the seasonal flowers introduces autumn thus:

The Michaelmas Daisies, among dede weeds,
Blooms for S. Michael's valourous deeds;
And seems the last of floures that stode,
Till the feste of S. Simon and S. Jude –
Save Mushrooms, and the Fungus race,
That grow till All-Hallow-tide takes place.
Soon the evergreen Laurel alone is greene,
When Catherine crownes all learned menne,
The Ivie and Holly Berries are seen,
And Yule Long and Wassaile come round again.

St. Michael was known in the ancient Celtic Christian church as Michael nam Buadh, the conquering angel who cast the Devil into Hell. The myth continues that the Devil landed first in blackberry bushes and in rural counties it was said that the Devil had stamped on the fruit and that it was extremely ill-advised to gather blackberries after Michaelmas, September 29th. The Michaelmas goose was usually the centrepiece of the festive table, served with the late autumn vegetables, cabbage, leeks and parsnips, and decorated with roast spiced apples.

As autumn turns to winter, so the souls of the dearly departed were thought to return to earth to warm themselves at the hearth fires of their loved ones and to partake once again in the love and community they had enjoyed while alive. But it was not just the good ghostly spirits of friends and family that returned; also goblins, witches, frights and haints revisited the earth to wreak mischief and havoc. I remember staying as a child at an aunt's house in the Kilkenny countryside around the time of All Hallow's Eve; in hushed tones she warned me that not only would the leprechauns be out and about that night, but the fairies would be running through the countryside trying to lure the unwary to follow them into the hills with promises that their life's treasure would be revealed. Those that were gullible enough to follow were never seen again! (In other words, be grateful for what you have here and now.)

Native to the New World, the bright orange jack-o'-lantern pumpkin had yet to be discovered when folk started making ghoulish faces on hollowed-out turnips to scare away goblins and witches. The tradition of trick or treat harks back to the idea of placating evil spirits with offerings of food and drink, like the bowlfuls of oats and milk placed on the doorstep to satisfy the hunger of returning spirits. However, All Souls' Day, which falls on the second day of November also had a tradition of 'souling' when the poor were permitted to beg from door to door for alms in the way that the unhappy souls of the dead returned on that day to seek solace among the living.

In Celtic tradition, November 1st marked Samhain and the return of winter. Bonfires were lit to symbolically fend off the coming chill. On November 5th, more bonfires are lit in England to mark Guy Fawkes Night when an effigy of the man who tried to blow up the Houses of Parliament is burned atop a huge pyre. On November 11th in France the feast of Martinmas honouring St. Martin, the patron of beggars and outcasts, is celebrated by people carrying candle lanterns through the darkened houses and streets – symbolizing the light and hope brought by St. Martin.

Finally, the cycle of autumn festivals concludes with Thanksgiving Day, celebrated on the third Thursday of November wherever there are Americans and they can roast a turkey. This unique holiday has, wherever it is observed, introduced one of America's greatest desserts to the culinarily deprived of the world – pumpkin pie! Love it or hate it, it's more American than apple pie, and twice as filling.

Before I began raising delicate little 'Sugar Pie' pumpkins in my English garden, I had to depend on tinned purée purchased at huge expense from the food hall at Harrods department store in London. Pumpkin growing has become something of a cult as British gardeners become increasingly aware that there is a huge variety of shape, colour and

ABOVE *The ruby red hips of* Rosa *'Scabrosa' appear in early autumn, while the shrub continues to throw plenty of bright pink, spicy-scented flowers among the golden yellow autumn-coloured foliage. Rose hips can be used to make a sweet jelly or syrup that is rich in vitamin C, and a jelly made of apple and hips flavoured with savoury herbs like tarragon or thyme makes an especially fine condiment to serve with roast meat or poultry.*

flavour among pumpkins. In France and Italy there are several pale-skinned sorts with mild, sweet-flavoured flesh; the vast, flat, deep orange variety 'Rouge Vif d'Etampes' resembles the pumpkin Cinderella used to get to the ball and is used to make the delicious *potage au potiron*, a classic of Orléanais cuisine. There is a dove-grey sort that is extremely popular in New Zealand and Australia (where friends tell me pumpkin is the national vegetable, appearing regularly on every barbecue).

HARVEST SOUP

In October, the field pumpkins return to the roadside stands, waiting to be selected for jack-o'-lantern carving; it's great fun searching for the Perfect Pumpkin, and even more fun eating the soup that can be prepared from the flesh once Halloween is over. I make this soup by cutting the vegetable into large chunks, peeling them with a sharp knife, tossing them in olive oil, salt and pepper, and then roasting in the oven until soft enough to pass through a *mouli légume*, which is preferable to using a food processor; the purée will be silky smooth. An alternative to roasting is to steam the pieces in the microwave to conserve the flavour and texture.

In a large saucepan, soften a large chopped onion and one large clove of garlic in about 25g (1oz) of butter. Add one tablespoon of white wine to moisten, before pouring in 500ml (1pt) of chicken stock. Simmer a few minutes before adding 1l (2pt) of puréed pumpkin; if the mix is too stiff, add more stock or wine to thin it to the preferred consistency. Season with salt, pepper and one teaspoon of toasted

and ground cumin seeds (toast the seeds in a dry frying pan until the aroma is released). Sprinkle with fresh chopped coriander/cilantro leaf before serving.

While researching recipes for *The Art of the Kitchen Garden*, I came across a pie recipe in an English cookery book of 1685, titled *The Accomplish't Cook*, written by Robert May. This is a savoury rather than a sweet pie in which the pumpkin is coarsely chopped, mixed with eggs and flavoured with thyme, rosemary and marjoram, as well as cinnamon, nutmeg and cloves – which in the seventeenth century were expensive spices. The mix was fried and then layered in the pie crust with sliced apples and raisins over which a custard of egg yolks and white wine was poured to set the whole thing in cooking. Given the exotic spices and

ABOVE *Pumpkins and other winter squash are among the most colourful and decorative denizens of the autumn garden. Pumpkins are the mascot of the season, for making jack-o'-lanterns in October, pumpkin pie in November and warming soups and pastas dishes during winter.*

the complexity of the recipe, pumpkin did at one time enjoy a certain popularity, probably because of its novelty value as a New World import. But the basic mix, with or without spices and possibly leaving out the raisins and definitely the apple, bears a reasonable resemblance to the traditional filling for *Ravioli di Zucca*, pumpkin ravioli. The best pumpkin to use for this would be the Antipodean grey-skinned sort as it is firm and has a lower water content than other

sorts. Sage goes well with pumpkin, too, and is part of the traditional Italian recipe, as is a handful of grated parmesan.

PUMPKIN PIE

The classic sweet pie mix is a custard made by combining 3 lightly beaten eggs with 225g (8oz) of sugar, 1 teaspoon of salt and mixed spice. Scald 225ml (8fl oz) of milk and 115ml (4fl oz) of double/heavy cream. Stir it slowly into the egg mixture, and then add 225g (8oz) of puréed pumpkin. Blend well until evenly mixed and pour into a pre-baked 23cm (9in) pie crust and bake at 200°C/400°F/gas 6 for the first ten minutes, reducing the heat to 170°C/325°F/gas 3 for a further 20–25 minutes, or until a knife inserted in the middle comes out clean. The pie filling will crack and brown around the edges, and the centre will be glossy and slightly tacky to the touch. Serve *à la mode*, with generous scoops of real vanilla ice cream. Forget the turkey and trimmings!

KNOW AND LOVE YOUR SQUASH

Pumpkins are just one sort of winter squash, and all squash are members of the Cucurbitaceae family. It is a huge group and includes the familiar sorts like courgette/zucchini, acorn squash, and little flying-saucer-shaped patty pan squash with the crimped edges, as well as the weirder crook-neck squash, butternut squash, spaghetti squash (steam in the microwave and serve with fresh tomato sauce), and warty-skinned Hubbard squash. Summer squash are eaten in summer (surprise!) when the skin is soft and the fruit immature; winter squash are eaten from autumn through winter, since they are mostly hard shelled and so can be stored. Some winter squash have extremely hard skins, but if you cut along the 'seam' or longitudinal ridge, you can generally gain access to the flesh and the seeds. Incidentally, don't throw away pumpkin seeds, roast and salt them instead; they are very nourishing. Soak first in water for about an hour to release them from the gooey fibres.

Baked acorn squash is delicious prepared with 1 tablespoon of butter and brown sugar nestled in the scooped-out middle; any squash can be prepared this way, or roasted as described for pumpkin. Serve roasted pumpkin with a balsamic vinegar dressing as part of a *salade tiède,* or warm salad. In her book *Chez Panisse Vegetables*, Alice Waters gives some of the best winter squash recipes including one for risotto made with a chicken stock base and diced butternut squash flavoured with sage, white wine and finished with parmesan and butter. Leave the finished risotto in the covered pan for ten minutes before serving; it helps to 'cure'.

PRESERVES, CONSERVES AND KEEPING THE HARVEST

One corner of my grandmother's basement in Milwaukee, Wisconsin was lined with Kilner jars and earthenware crocks filled with apple butters, sauerkraut, bread 'n' butter pickles, bottled beets, mustard beans, and other comestibles that she produced from her regular harvesting of the Farmer's Market, downtown. She was not a vegetable gardener herself, although she grew her own dill and chives and some other herbs. Her expertise was in the kitchen, and anyone who could make a cabbage taste that good was expert indeed. But because I chose to grow my own, the conserving of the harvest had to be reduced to a minimum, so I relied on the microwave and the freezer. If it would freeze – and most vegetables will – I would first slice, dice or otherwise prepare the vegetables and then zap on high (mine was an 800W oven) for about 3 minutes, about 225g (8oz) at a time with just the water that clung to the veg after cleaning. Spreading the vegetable in an even layer in a shallow pyrex dish and covering with a special microwave dish cover seemed to work really well. But it was critical to transfer the vegetables to a sinkful of very cold water the minute they came out of the oven. This stops the cooking process so the flesh would not go squishy. Then they must be drained as fully as possible to prevent ice crystals forming. To freeze, you can spread them on baking sheets or special freezer trays, then bag and label once frozen. Open freezing makes the vegetables 'pourable' instead of congealed in one solid mass of ice.

To deal with the tomato glut and avoid hours stirring steaming pink sludge, you can microwave the harvest, or roast it. Cut each fruit in half and scoop out the watery seeds in the middle. Pack in a single layer in a non-stick baking pan and put in a hot oven until the cut edges begin to brown. Let the roasted toms cool down before puréeing in a *mouli légume*; the pulp will pass through but the skins

RIGHT *Drying flowers for decoration is one of autumn's more pleasing tasks.*

will be left behind to toss on the compost heap.

Sweetcorn can be frozen the moment it is picked, husks and all. It is cold work removing the outer leaves, but wear gloves. You'll find the hairs come away easily.

HERBAL HARVEST

The kitchen garden is not the only place where autumn's bounty can be found; many of the herbs are highly ornamental plants and now is the time to gather in branches of rosemary, thyme, tarragon, marjoram and other shrubby herbs.

Some herbs, like thyme and marjoram, can be cut back to bristly clumps; tarragon can be shaved to the ground, while some care must be taken with rosemary as in cold climates the plant needs some protection for its branches.

Tie the gathered branches together in small bundles or else spread them over a drying rack made by stretching cheesecloth or muslin across a wooden frame. Leave in a shady spot where the air circulates freely to dry slowly and evenly. Under the bed can be a good place (if you are dust conscious and keep that area clear!). Otherwise, hang the bunches from an indoor clothesline. I have dried rosemary and thyme successfully in the microwave by putting the branches on a paper towel to absorb the moisture that is given off. But be careful not to burn the herbs; remember they have oil in their leaves.

Drying soft-leaved herbs like parsley and coriander is less successful in my experience, so to have 'fresh' green leaves on hand, I rinse them in clean water, shake out the access and put in freezer bags. The leaves will shatter the first time you scoop some out, but it's rather like having instant chopped herbs ready to flavour stews and soups. You can also freeze chopped herbs in ice-stock-cubes; a teaspoon or so of the herb per cube section and then fill the tray with fresh stock.

LEFT *Other seedheads are valuable in the autumn garden. The silky seedheads of* Clematis orientalis *are among the best.*

RIGHT *The emerald pods of* Agapanthus *last well in the border and look well among ornamental grasses.*

ABOVE *Some seedheads are particularly dark and distinctive, like those of the purple coneflower,* Echinacea purpurea.

RIGHT *The dark tones of angelica umbels and the seed-bearing whorls of* Phlomis fruticosa *are silhouetted against pale plumes of the grass* Calamagrostis × acutiflora *'Karl Foerster'.*

This is better than using plain water as the addition of a frozen herb cube won't water down the dish you are preparing. This is also a good way to conserve pot marigold (*Calendula officinalis*) petals.

The bright yellow marigold petals were known as the poor cook's saffron, for the bright colouring they impart to a dish, and the warm, softly spicy flavour they lend to broths. Next time you poach or coddle an egg, sprinkle a few calendula petals over the top; the white will colour as if saffron threads had been added.

POT POURRI

Marigold petals dry really well for use in the kitchen or in pot pourri, one of the oldest dried flower concoctions still in use today. Lavender and rose petals are the main ingredients in pot pourri, which translates as rotten pot and is so-called because the earliest mixes were moist with perfumed oils and kept in covered jars. The lid would be removed to release the scent and to top up the mix with fresh petals as needed.

Other flower petals used are violets, heliotrope, mignonette, sweet woodruff and pinks. The foliage used is predominantly citrus-scented, like lemon verbena, lemon

balm, and any of the scented-leaf geraniums. Box leaves, and kitchen herbs like rosemary, thyme and sage fill out the mix and the perfumes are 'fixed' or preserved by stirring in a blend of cinnamon, nutmeg, whole cloves, mace and violet-scented orris root powder, prepared from the dried root of the Florentine iris, *Iris florentina*. Essential oils are added too, a few drops now and then – patchouli and sandalwood lending a seductive note; while flower oils make a lighter scented pot pourri. Salt is used to make a moist pot pourri as it prevents mould and stops the petals actually rotting down to an odoriferous compost – use coarse sea salt or kosher rock salt.

Gather flowers in the morning just as the dew is dried from the petals, and spread them to dry as described for herbs. Have ready a large earthenware crock with a lid or other container with a tight fitting lid. Add the flowers and foliage in layers with the salt and the spice and orris root mix. To 450g (1lb) of flowers and foliage add roughly 50g (2oz) of orris root and a tablespoon of each spice used. To make a moist pot pourri, add 75–100g (3–4oz) of salt mixed with the spice blend of choice in between 1cm (1/2in) layers of flower and foliage. Leave tightly sealed for ten days, then decant into a large bowl and mix well.

I have a huge bowl of pot pourri to which, over the years, I have added flowers and leaves from our garden and from the bouquets my husband has given me marking, so far, each of the twenty years of our marriage. The bowl serves up my life story in a way, brimming as it is with love and memories, to be added to with scented leaves and flowers from my Texas garden.

SAVE A SEED, SAVE A PENNY

Cottage gardeners were frugal gardeners; not for them the yearly purchase of expensive packets of hybrid seed. Instead they left a part of every crop, be it vegetable or floral, to ripen on the stem to provide them with the wherewithal for next year's harvest. Following in their tradition can save you a few pennies as well as adding a wealth of texture and shape to the autumn garden.

As I have already mentioned, on occasions too numerous to list, don't rush to tidy up in autumn. Instead, take the time to mark the flowers that really knocked your socks off; the vegetables that were especially good to grow and eat. Tie a tiny string around the plants so you know which flower to aim for, and as the seed ripens keep an eye on it to gather in the capsules before they burst. This will only work if the seed you are earmarking is from species plants or old-fashioned 'heritage' plants, garden forms that have not been the subject of the hybridists' improvements (I don't know that a grossly double, pompon hollyhock or poppy is necessarily more desirable than a simple old-fashioned single, where each part of the flower is clearly defined and the colour shines true and bright).

LEFT *Let your autumn garden go to seed; it what the season is all about and you will be rewarded with some pretty effects and plenty of self-sown seedlings to pot up and share with fellow gardeners. Here, Stachys byzantina 'Cotton Boll' makes showy fuzzy spikes against a background of angel's fishing rods, Dierama pulcherrimum, and Gypsophila paniculata 'Schneeflocke'.*

There is no hard and fast rule about when seed is ripe for gathering, it is simply a case of look and learn. Some seed capsules literally explode when the seed is ripe; among them dill, caraway, fennel, hardy geraniums and euphorbias. So keep an eye on the plant and when the pod begins to darken, snip it from the plant with a length of stem intact and put into a paper envelope. Label clearly and then set the envelopes in a dry warm spot. The pod will ripen and spit its seed into the container.

On legume pods, and that includes lupins and sweet peas as well as beans, wait until the pod looks like the shell has been shrink-wrapped around the seed inside. Then gather them up, set somewhere to dry for a few days and then shell the seed just as you would shell the fresh vegetable.

Martagon lily pods and iris pods tend to split open exposing the seed and then slowly unfold until wide open when the breeze catches the papery lily seed or birds peck out the iris seed, depositing them 'naturally' as they are digested.

Some seed comes with feathery attachments or chaff that is hard to separate from the seed; other seed is just plain painful to gather like thistle or coneflower seed. The latter can be done easily by putting the entire dried flowerhead in a paper sack and wait for the seed to drop out naturally. You can gently roll it around to help the process. Don't bother to remove the chaffy bits if you are going to sow the seed in your own garden, the seed will germinate anyway. But if you are going to use the seed for barter, then clean it up first.

THE LASTING
FRAMEWORK

The lumpen snow-covered shapes in my friend's Boston garden could be said to be adding shape and form to the winter garden scene, just as the shapes and textures of the shrubs and trees supporting the snow make the autumn view of her garden more interesting. It is not just the colour of foliage or the brightness of the flowers that will make the autumn garden a beautiful sight to behold, it is also the contribution they can make as boundaries, eye-catchers, screens and sculpture that define the garden throughout the year, as well as being of major significance in autumn and winter.

HEDGES

Gardens are not natural; one of the most evident changes a gardener makes to the natural terrain is by planting hedges which, apart from prehistoric earthworks, are probably the oldest artificial feature in the landscape. Hedges defined the perimeters of a village, of an individual property, or separated the vegetable garden from the stock yard. Most often hedges were planted using saplings scavenged from the wild or else grown from wild-gathered seed. One of the earliest descriptions of hedge planting details how it could be easily done by impregnating a length of twisted hemp rope with the seed of hedgerow plants. Laying the rope in the trench where the hedge was needed, it was watered well and regularly. It was kept weed free and the seedlings were quickly established. Traditionally, hedges were planted on top of ditches; the owner of the ditch owned the hedge since the soil for the ditch was thrown back onto his property, and the hedge was planted on top of the mounded soil.

My garden in rural Norfolk was bounded on two sides by a hedge that was at least 150 years old. There were magnificent crab apple trees (great for making herb jellies in autumn), bullace plums, holly, hazelnut trees, elders and field maples. Throughout the year the hedge was vibrant with flowers, fruit, birds, rabbits, foxes, owls and numerous butterflies and other beneficial insects. There was also one old apple tree of a variety called 'Arthur Turner', still producing huge cooking apples, but with old age its yield was gradually lessening.

With a back drop like that against which to plant a garden from scratch, I was bound to use the venerable old hedge as the leading inspiration for any new hedge planting I undertook. Ultimately, I had a mix of hedges dividing a large unruly cottage garden into specific planting areas. There were clipped linear evergreen hedges in dwarf box

ABOVE *Peacock shapes are probably the the oldest motifs in the art of topiary. This is the Peacock Garden at Great Dixter.*

PREVIOUS PAGE *At the gardens at the Old Vicarage near the North Sea coast of Norfolk, strictly disciplined hedges divide the garden into distinct rooms, but most importantly provide much needed shelter and help to create the micro-climates the extensive plant collections need to survive. The perfectly clipped topiary reinforces the vistas and ornaments the avenues of this extensive formal garden.*

around a small formal lawn and a 2.4m (8ft) tall yew 'excedra', a sweeping curve of midnight green that separated the ornamental flower garden from the wilderness of orchard and hazelnut walk beyond. The tall hornbean hedge around the formal flower borders gradually transformed into a

mixed 'tapestry' hedge as it came to enclose the orchard and wild garden areas. Near the house were hedges of sweetbriar and rugosa roses to scent the evening air, along with lavender and catmint. In their maturity, the garden hedges matched the character of their setting and the garden benefited from the protection the old field hedge gave the beds and borders.

PATIENCE IS A VIRTUE

I firmly believe that the biggest mistake people make when planting a hedge is to use 'fast-growing' shrubs. It is false economy. Lawson's cypress is especially evil as I know from bad experience; the builder who did the conversion to make the old barn into a house planted a mixed bag of these fast-growing evergreens. I always meant to dig them out, but never got around to it. At first I thought the fact he had

planted them in their black poly-bag pots would be enough to kill them (always let it be said, 'Remove pots before planting'), but I had not bargained on the tenacious grip these things put on life. Away they grew, and the more I trimmed and topped (which I admit was infrequently – there being so many other things to do) the larger and faster they grew. Now they are the new owner's problem, and I am truly sorry.

However, I am doing penance with the hedges around my Texas garden. Like so many American gardeners, the inclination is to plant something evergreen around the house. So I have acquired from previous owners an unhealthy blend of privet, Burford holly, and aphid-covered euonymus, all planted hard up against the foundations, which I'm certain is not what the well-known US landscaping feature 'foundation planting' is meant to be.

I know it to be a myth that evergreens like yew and box are slow growing – the reason gardeners usually give for not planting them. The excedra in my English garden was a 7.5m (25ft) curve of luscious dense green that had reached its height of 2.4m (8ft) just seven years after planting. It regularly put on 45cm (18in) of growth in the first few years and then slowed to 25–30cm (10–12in) because once it was established and growing well, I stopped feeding it. And I did not begin the hedge with 1.2m (4ft) tall plants, choosing instead to use 60cm (2ft) tall rooted cuttings, which were considerably cheaper. Other yew hedges in the garden were raised from seedlings transported from the yew grove at a friend's property in Kent. The seedlings were also about 60cm (2ft) tall and soon caught up thanks to regular feeding and watering. Similarly, the dwarf box hedging started out as fist-sized rooted cuttings planted on 30cm (1ft) centres. I have to admit that it took me a few seasons to believe that they were actually growing, but within five years they had knitted together to form a dense frame for the formal lawn.

It is no secret that if you water and feed, the plants will grow. My regime for the yews and box was to feed with a quite high nitrogen fertilizer (pelleted chicken manure or, if you can get it, Peruvian bat guano!) in the early spring just as things were beginning to wake up. Then I took care to water well throughout the summer, applying a general purpose, balanced fertilizer like Growmore, in midsummer. The same regime worked for the hornbeam hedges and the tapestry hedge, while the lavender and roses received a general feed during summer and were mulched with rotted compost along with the rest of the garden.

Late summer and early autumn is the time to prune and clip yew hedges and most deciduous ones; take care to clip with sloping sides or 'batter', so that the hedge is wider at the base than at the top. In the first few years the aim is to create shape and bulk; after that you must remove the new growth to retain the shape and prevent the shrubs outgrowing the confines of the desired hedge height and girth (my inherited hedges are buffeting the gutters having long ago over-reached the foundations! But I'm told things are supposed to be bigger in Texas).

Incidentally, a tapestry hedge is one which is made up of all sorts of different hedging plants; in England the most famous tapestry hedge is at Hidcote Manor Gardens in Gloucestershire, where the creator of the garden, an American expatriate, used a blend of hollies, yew, box and hornbeam to divide the garden into a series of rooms, each quite different in character from the other. One of the best times of year to visit this garden is in the autumn when the hedges are turning and the foliage and flowers present a marvellous selection of seasonal colour.

KNOTS AND OTHER CLIPPINGS

Patterns made of lightly clipped dwarf hedges, planted with colourful flowers or filled with coloured stones, have the appearance of oriental carpets laid on the garden ground. Frank Lawley, who is an expert on oriental carpets and one of England's finest plantsmen has a theory that this is indeed how this decorative device first came into being. Knot gardens were hugely popular during the Tudor period; Henry VIII had a huge collection of oriental carpets, some 'inherited' from the ill-fated Cardinal Wolsey, while others were no doubt purchased from Venetian tradesmen who were importing these fabulous textiles from Persia and the Orient. Portraits of the period often show oriental carpets in the background. So it seems a quite natural extension to take the motifs, translate them into hedge and flower and spread them in the garden below the best rooms of the manor house or palace. During every season of the year, the knot would give something pleasing for the eye to rest upon.

Contemporary knot gardeners can use abstract motifs to create the pattern or fall back on traditional designs; these are easily found as a number of gardening books over the past ten years have included plans and details, including my own book *Herb Garden Design*. Knots are ideal for small courtyard gardens where formality is required. The small beds formed by the interweaving hedges can be planted with bulbs, annuals and perennials to allow a varied display throughout the year. It is standard practice, too, to clip the shrubs before they flower, which has always seemed a pity to me, since the lemon-curd yellow buttons of *Santolina pinnata* ssp. *neapolitana* 'Edward Bowles' are quite pretty; and all the herbs flower prolifically, attracting bees and butterflies to decorate the knot. So, ever the iconoclast, I never pruned my knot, described below, until the early autumn, by which time it was looking distinctly un-knotted. However, that to me is part of the charm of autumn gardens.

Dwarf box (*Buxus sempervirens* 'Suffruticosa') has been the plant of choice for most knot gardeners over the years, but gardening texts from the sixteenth and seventeenth centuries list herb shrubs like hyssop, rosemary, thyme, lavender and southernwood as possibilities for knot-planting. In Italy during this time, small flowers like the lawn daisy were popular to lay out temporary patterns, while pinks, sea thrift and other clumping groundcovers were also popular. In my Norfolk garden, I had, in addition to the dwarf box lawn edging, a knot of sorts; it was more free-form than based on any historical model, and planted with hyssop and the evergreen *Santolina rosmarinifolia* ssp. *rosmarinifolia*, framed with grey leaf southernwood. In his Northumberland garden at Herterton House, Frank Lawley has planted

a physic garden using pink-flowered *Saxifraga* 'Clarence Elliott' to edge the central beds of the herbal knot, while the side beds are framed with white-flowered sea thrift. Were I to plant a knot in my Texas garden (perhaps using a lasso or half-hitch as a motif?) I would be tempted to try dwarf yaupon holly combined with *Rosmarinus officinalis* 'Tuscan Blue' and the excellent *Lavandula* 'Sawyers'. There are, by the way, two forms of knot: Lawley's knot garden is an open-knot since the paths that cut through it allow you walk on the floral carpet. Closed knots are ones where the pattern can only be viewed from outside the knot.

Knot gardens planted with perennials can be tided up in autumn and mulched to give a neat appearance during winter, or if you are going to bed out the knot for seasonal interest, clear away the summer show to make way for bulbs and winter-hardy annuals.

TOTALLY OVER THE TOPIARY

Tudor gardens must have been incredibly lively to look at, what with all the knots, mazes, and gilt and polychromed garden ornaments that decorated the space. In the background of a portrait of Henry VIII's family there is a small glimpse of a garden, complete with raised flower beds edged with narrow rails painted with green and white diagonal stripes and garnished at the corners with wooden sculptures of the King's Beasts (unicorns, dragons, etc). These are painted white, red and other pure colours and highlighted with glittering gold gilt (also present is one of Henry's oriental carpets). It is said that these sculpted ornaments are what

inspired early English topiary: geometric and figurative shapes clipped in box and yew. Another thought is that Crusaders, having seen peacocks and other oddities in the Near East, embellished their manor gardens with shrubby representations of the exotica they had encountered. This sounds just about as fanciful as the topiary itself.

Like a hedge that lends structure to a dormant garden during the late autumn and throughout winter, topiary shapes provide a visual anchor in the landscape, although some might say 'blot', as I discovered in 1987 when researching *English Topiary Gardens*; it seems there is no gray area with topiary, people either love it or hate it. William Robinson was a hater; in his scheme of things – wild and natural gardens – topiary was an abhorrent aberration. Topiary had been around a long time before that, at least since it featured in early Roman gardens in Italy and its outposts (including Britain), and it may well predate that by some millennia – there are representations of clipped trees in ancient Egyptian papyri. But topiary really reached a zenith

LEFT *Clipped box and holly define the knot garden beds at the Old Vicarage. Each bed is filled with bold-coloured annual flowers and foliage that carries the garden through to first frost.*

RIGHT *A simple pot filled with the spiky grey foliage and clove-scented flowers of dianthus draws the eye toward the planting behind, where* Aster novi-belgii *'Winston S. Churchill' and* A. *'Coombe Fishacre' mingle with the* Dahlia *'Helga' and little blue flowers of* Ceratostigma willmottianum.

of popularity in the Arts and Crafts gardens of Edwardian England, and soon spread to the Colonial revival gardens of the eastern USA. In Europe and wherever Italianate gardens were built there would be topiary incorporated into the miles of box edging that created the 'garden rooms'.

Because of its artificial nature, topiary is most often found in formal gardens, reinforcing the architecture of the garden with a design vocabulary that includes tetrahedrons, spheres, cones, pyramids, peacocks, teapots and teddybears. Such shapes mark the corners of informally planted herbaceous borders, or divide the planting space of herb gardens into spoke wheels and sheltering bays. Wherever zoomorphic topiary appears, it is usually the result of a fertile imagination let loose on an innocent box tree. 'That branch sticking out just seemed to suggest a peacock tail', or 'The hedge had got rather lumpy, and began to look like the Loch Ness Monster', are how two gardeners once described their inspiration to me.

Just as autumn is the ideal time to plant a hedge, hardy shrubs destined to be topiaried should be also be planted now. Because the shrub or shrubs will be in place for a very long time, they will be making extra demands on soil fertility so prepare the ground generously, incorporating plenty of well-rotted compost or manure and make sure that the drainage is adequate. If the soil is very heavy add gravel or grit; compost will improve the water-holding properties of sandy soil.

When purchasing box and yew plants for either hedges, knots or topiary, try to obtain ones that have been raised

LEFT *At the Bois des Moutiers, an autumn garden huddles around a sundial. The house was built during the Arts and Crafts period in the early 1900s by the English architect Edwin Lutyens. Sundial gardens were a favourite motif of his (he often designed the hardscape as well) and of gardeners generally during this time. Sundials hark back to the historic gardens of Tudor England and Renaissance Italy, which were the model for so many Arts and Crafts garden designers, and were the focal point of hedge-enclosed garden rooms. The inscriptions were usually melancholic, referring to the transcience of life and the gardener's mortality: 'Thou seest the hour, but knowest not the hour'. In the autumn the garden life cycle comes full circle, so what could be more appropriate?*

from the same stock, in the case of cutting-raised material, as box can vary in leaf colour and size and yew raised from seed can be extremely variable and would give an uneven appearance to what is meant to be a uniform feature.

Lollipop or mop-head standards are popular for container-grown topiary and can often be purchased ready-shaped. Rosemary, bay (*Laurus nobilis*), scented-leaf geraniums, patio roses, lemon verbena as well as common box (*Buxus sempervirens*) are often seen as the central feature in urns and other formal containers. Often these plants will only survive if brought indoors during winter. Indeed, in cold climates, the key to success with half-hardy shrubs like lemon verbena and scented-leaf geraniums is to over-winter them in a frost-free place and to stop watering until early spring when they should be encouraged out of dormancy and pruned of the previous year's growth.

MAKE MINE A MICRO-CLIMATE

One last word about the importance of hedges and screens in the garden – in autumn or otherwise – is that careful

LEFT *A rustic gazebo made of hazel wands stands out in its nakedness in an early autumn border, but by the end of the season as the garden loses its colour and the trees their foliage, it will blend in unnoticably.*

RIGHT *A beautifully observed sculpture of a soaring red kite, a rare Welsh bird of prey, graces the autumnal garden, reminding us that the seasons fly by on silent wings.*

positioning can help you garden by creating micro-climates within the overall garden. Just as the old field hedge protected my English garden in rural Norfolk from the prevailing southwest wind, so the hornbeam hedge sheltered the perennial border in front of it from the freezing fogs and gales that blew in off the North Sea, straight from the Urals. So, for most Norfolk gardens, and other gardens where wind is a major feature, establishing shelter belt protection is of prime importance. And within the garden hedges can be used to further increase zones of relative stillness.

You can also exploit the natural micro-climates that occur in your garden. In cold climates, notice where the early morning sun first strikes; this will be the first spot to warm and not a good place to put plants that flower early, since the quick thaw would damage delicate plant tissues. Put them instead on a southwest-facing aspect so that they

ABOVE *Boldly planted containers using tender exotics are at their best in autumn. The centrepiece of this urn is* Agave americana.

warm up gently. Early summer-flowering plants can often be ruined by a snap late frost, so put them against a cooler northwest-facing aspect so that flowering is held back until the frosts are truly over. Similarly, a thick blanket of mulch laid in the autumn over early flowering perennials or bulbs helps to keep them tucked up underground until the danger of frost damage is over.

Colour can affect the relative warmth in a garden; in vegetable gardens, a black plastic mulch warms up the soil more quickly than a clear plastic cloche. The effect of burning a prairie is to leave a deposit of black stubble on the soil which then warms more rapidly, so helping prairie plant seed to germinate. Hard-landscaping materials can have the same effect: a brick wall stores heat, which is why fruit trees are often trained against them; paving stones too can store heat that radiates into the soil around to help marginal rock plants through frosty weather.

Understand the lay of the land. A frost pocket will form at the lowest point on sloping ground because cold air flows downhill, even the bottom of a south-facing slope will be the last place to warm-up in the garden while the top of the slope will be quickly warm. So think about where you are naturalizing those narcissi and early spring bulbs.

In warm climates the trick is to provide pockets of cool shade, so dividing a wide open sunny space – like my new garden – with a series of low hedges or vine-covered trellis will enlarge the plant palette. I'm even thinking about putting topiary to work, and 'cloud-pruning' an evergreen shrub to shade our air conditioner unit, which unfortunately is located against a southwest-facing wall.

POTS AND PATHS

Container gardens are for those of us without a 'grounded' garden, like my friend Lee, whose garden is on the roof top of his four-floor building in downtown Manhattan. It is his pride and joy and, being an interior designer, gives him the opportunity to stretch his talent for exterior decor. Lee observes the changing seasons by tending his carefully amassed collection of very large, very simple containers, all of which are painted black. Some of these are permanently planted with silver-leaved shrubs and deciduous trees, including a white-barked silver birch. Along the low parapet wall he has trained a white-flowered wisteria; all the perennials are white-flowered and the seasonal bulbs and annuals are also white. In the summer, when foliage and flower are in full fettle, the dark containers disappear and the impression is of a cool leafy glade, only two blocks from Macy's on 7th Avenue. By October, Lee is beginning the winterizing process; clearing the perennial 'beds' of faded top-growth, removing wilted summer bedding and adding a few more bulbs for spring colour beneath the trees. Some pots are brought indoors, others are heavily mulched with straw.

In England during early autumn, I would bring the standard lemon verbenas into the greenhouse, as well as the scented-leaf geraniums and collection of succulent plants that spent the fine weather of spring and summer on a sunny, south-facing step. I generally tried to tidy these up, with the exception of the verbena, which kept its old growth until the spring, by removing dead stems and faded leaves. Any plants that had outgrown their containers were repotted, so that in spring they received no check to new growth by being disturbed. Many of the most useful container plants are half-hardy, such as the highly colourful coleus, gazania, sweet potato vine (*Ipomoea batatas*) in dark purple or lime green, *Plectranthus*, *Agastache*, cardoon, *Eucomis* and *Phormium*, because they continue putting on a fine show right up to first frosts. They can be increased by taking cuttings in late summer into early autumn, or by making divisions or potting on offsets.

Autumn is the time for maintenance work on containers. Too often we forget that the fabric of the garden requires attention if it is to play its supporting role in the unfolding drama of the seasons. As you repot container plants, inspect the old pots for cracks and dings. Unless they are priceless urns, it is really not worth keeping them, better to bust them up to use as crocks to provide adequate drainage in the bottom of new containers. Those you are keeping should be brushed out and then washed in a solution of warm water and household disinfectant to clean off algae. Plastic containers can become brittle over time and exposure to bright sunlight, so assess the durability of any you are using. Wooden half-barrels may be rotting and so offer an invitation to insect pests. Are there any ant colonies establishing in permanently planted containers of ornamental shrubs? Their tunnelling exposes the roots to more air than they require and will eventually kill the plant, so get the ants first by watering in an ant-specific pesticide.

In his book *Garden Paths*, Vermont-based garden designer, Gordon Hayward, clearly sets out the design and construction of what is ultimately the most important landscape feature. As he says, 'The path… is far more than a means of getting from here to there on dry, solid ground. It is a way to organise your thinking about garden design: it is a way to organise space and clarify the meaning of your whole garden… . It invites, even pulls people into the garden. To look at a garden in terms of its paths, then is to look

along the path edges into the flower beds. Rake it over and spread new mulch to keep up the levels. Brick and concrete paths that pass through shady parts of the garden can become slippery with moss and algae, so wash them down with a good stiff brush and a de-mossing solution. Similarly, wooden decks or duckboarding will not last forever, so check them for damage.

If paths are the main arteries of the garden, then the potting shed is the nerve centre, and autumn is a good time to clear out the previous year's old seed packets, broken pots, squashed seed trays, tangled twine and cobwebs so that, come the spring, the synapses will be snapping freely as you spring to work. Clean all pots and seed trays with disinfectant and stack neatly according to size; go through plant labels (the white plastic sort can be cleaned of old names by scrubbing lightly with an abrasive kitchen cleanser).

Check over all garden tools and clean off dirt that has encrusted around the handles. Oil and grease the moving parts and blades of cutting tools, and take the lawn mower to be serviced once you have given the grass its final cut of the year. Bring the hose indoors rather than leaving it to rot in the elements and check over the irrigation system in the kitchen garden – if you have such a system installed – otherwise, water butts can be emptied and cleaned. Just as we give the house a spring clean (don't we?), so we can give the garden its autumn clean. It helps to make your winter hibernation so much more relaxed knowing that for a while, at least, while enjoying some other favourite pastime, it is possible not to feel the pressure of garden work waiting to be

at the garden as whole, for it is the path that links all parts and thus helps create a sense of place.' So, take the time in autumn to clear the path (especially brick-laid or stone-paved paths) of weeds at the same time as you are weeding the flower beds. If the path is made of bark or wood mulch, pine needles or other organic material, it may have been worn bald or thin in places or the material may be 'leaking' done. During the off-season, I have always particularly enjoyed browsing through old gardening books, seeking inspiration or just generally musing on how very little things really do change over the centuries. One of my favourites is *Pot Pourri from a Surrey Garden*, written by Mrs C.W. Earle, a contemporary (and some say rival) of Gertrude Jekyll. She is so solidly down to earth with her comments and advice. Picking up her volume now, as autumn plays around my heels, I read, in the chapter devoted to September,

'In spite of all the charming things Mr [William] Robinson says about it, "wild gardening" is, I am sure, a delusion and a snare… it requires endless care, and is always extending in all directions in search of fresh soil. What is possible is to have the appearance of a wild garden in con-sequence of the most *judicious planting, with consummate knowledge and experience of the plants that will do well in the soil if they are just a little assisted at the time of planting'*. (My italics.)

She notices, too, the tameness of the robins as we dig over the soil, the dewy gossamer that hangs in the garden and the way the flowers shine out of the early mists as the low-angled autumn light strikes across the garden. She recalls, too, the remark of a friend whose garden is on England's east coast, maybe in Norfolk, for the comment is about how the wind will always scatter the autumn leaves before they have a chance to touch the ground. Feeling rather like those windblown leaves, I wonder, as I contem-plate the future as a gardener in Texas, will the memory of my English autumn garden ever fade? I doubt it.

LEFT & ABOVE *Each year at the Old Vicarage, Alan Gray makes masterful container displays using a wide range of fuchsias, solanums, geraniums, Eucomis, melianthus, and countless other exotics chosen for the vibrancy of their shape and colour. The fuchsia tower, right, is an assemblage of bicoloured pelargonium and scented geraniums, huddled around a huge urn planted with standard and trailing fuchsias. If you are going to container garden, be bold about it!*

GREAT AUTUMN PLANTS

There are all sorts of reasons to select a plant for the garden: maybe it has good foliage texture or the perfume is exciting; the shape might be unusual, the form architectural or the colour outstanding. When it comes to choosing a great autumn plant, however, colour is the single most relevant characteristic. In autumn, if the flowers are especially vivid, the berries bright, or the foliage adds a subtle range of hues to the fading fabric of the garden scheme, the plant gets noticed.

Plants in the natural landscape form layers; the tree canopy above the shrub and perennial layer, beneath which shelter the annuals, biennials, small bulbs and groundcover. How you manipulate nature in mixed borders or 'wild gardens', mindful all the while of suiting plants to site and each other, is how gardens are created. I hope that the plants described in the following pages will help you to add layers of colour to your garden in autumn, so that the passage of summer to winter turns likes the pages of a well-paced novel.

FOLIAGE

The layered planting of trees and shrubs comes vividly to life in autumn, composed as it is of a wide variety of differently sized and shaped plants which display their best colour just before leaf fall. Beneath the mottled grey trunk of a tall-growing eucalpytus (previous page), smaller, bright-leafed trees like Japanese dogwood, *Cornus kousa*, and paperbark maple, *Acer griseum*, cast their foliage over equally warm-hued medium-sized shrubs like wine-red *Berberis*. Ornamental grasses and low-growing shrubs including bridal wreath, *Spiraea japonica*, and grey-leafed *Brachyglottis greyii*, occupy the bottom layer of this mixed grouping. All these plants have a preference for moisture-retentive soil and slightly acid conditions, as well as having something else to offer, such as the dogwood's papery white bracts in spring, or the maple's year-long display of the cinnamon-red peeling bark (previous page inset).

Acer species and cultivars are the most rewarding for autumn garden-making; there is a huge number to choose from, some with fabulous colour or remarkable bark, or both. The intensity of the colour will vary with the region, being softer in mild climates.

Among the large-growing species, the silverleaf maple, *Acer saccharinum* (so-called for the silvery sheen of the underside of the leaves), and the common sycamore, *A. pseudoplatanus,* have little to recommend them other than quick growth – and the sycamore will self-sow anywhere and everywhere. The sugar maple, *A. saccharum*, is the typical tree of New England autumn colour scenes. It is

robustly hardy and grows to at least 35m (120ft), and so needs space to be shown off at its best. In smaller gardens and for purely ornamental purposes, the Japanese maples, cultivars of *A. palmatum*, are the ones to choose. These include small trees, some growing to about 9m (30ft) tall, with nicely shaped spreading crowns, as well as shrub-size or dwarf trees that form mounds of lacy foliage. These are the sort most frequently used as accent plants or among perennials in a mixed border. *A. p.* var. *dissectum* Dissectum Atropurpureum Group (above) is unquestionably the best known and most widely used for its finely divided dentate leaves that take on a deepening purple tone as the seasons progress.

A. p. 'Ôsakazuki' is a stalwart among the Japanese maples, with its flame-red autumn foliage. The cultivar A. p. 'Sango-kaku' has good yellow-coloured leaves that accentuate the coral-tinted bark; it is seen left, with the russet-red A. p. var. *dissectum*, and above, grown as a small grove. Young trees have the strongest coloured bark, but mature trees have an elegant shape with a broad spreading crown.

Some of the Japanese maples are desirable for their oddly shaped leaves; A. p. 'Okushimo' has a stiff upright habit and its lobed leaves seem to resemble the splayed pointy toes of some spindly bird's foot. A. p. 'Orido-Nishiki' has the prettiest variegation, with shades of pink, green, white and cream, changing through the seasons. A. p. 'Karasugawa' is almost entirely pink in leaf and stem, and the new growth is white stained with a rosy glow. It is not robust and requires shade and shelter, so is best suited to container growing.

Many of the other small-growing cultivars among the A. palmatum group are ideal for container growing. Use a potting mixture that will hold moisture well (since containers can quickly become arid zones!) and use a slow-release fertilizer to keep up levels of available nutrients.

Where winter temperatures drop below freezing it is advisable either to bring container-grown Japanese maples under cover, or else to insulate the containers by covering them in bubble wrap and a layer of hessian/burlap sacking.

Well-drained sandy loam, on the acid side of neutral, suits Japanese maples best. They are not deep rooting so mulching, especially in hot climates, will help to keep the roots moist in summer. In mild climates they do well in sun, although strong sun will scorch the leaves, so position plants where they will receive shade during the hottest part of the day.

Amelanchier canadensis (above), the service berry of North America and the snowy mespilus of Europe, deserves both common names for the good service it does in the garden all year round and the tiny white flowers of early spring. Held in loose clusters amid the ruddy brown-tinted foliage, the flowers look like late-falling snow, but by the beginning of autumn, the foliage is turning a vibrant flaming red-orange and the flowers have turned to berries which ripen from pale yellow to deep purple. Other species are equally attractive; *A. lamarckii* has silky juvenile foliage and the largest flower clusters, and most stunning autumn colour among the species. Native to the Allegheny mountains in northeastern America, these plants are fairly hardy and do best in neutral to acid soil in sun or part shade. They are suckering shrubs that can be grown as a small, multi-branched tree; they have a delicate gracefulness, and are ideally suited to small gardens.

Ampelopsis glandulosa var. *brevipedunculata* 'Elegans' (below) is less vigorous than some vines, only growing to about 3m (10ft). With its heavy mottling of cream and pink variegation, this tendril-climber needs a sheltered spot to prevent sunscorch, and in cold-zone gardens some protection against freezing. It can be used to clothe a low retaining wall or as ground-cover amongst shrubs and small trees which will provide the necessary shade and shelter; dark evergreens will provide a showcase background. The little specks of white are the juvenile fruit which mature to dark blue, adding another colour to the display. Any soil will suit, as long as it is moisture retentive.

Carya glabra (above) is commonly known as the pignut hickory and makes a tall-growing tree to 25m (80ft) with a prettily shaped conical crown in its early years. It has compound leaves of five lobes rather like those of its relative, the walnut; they turn to a fresh butter yellow in autumn. The pignut is more commonly seen in the eastern USA than the UK, but makes a fine specimen tree in either location. The nuts are not edible, so it might be an idea to grow a pignut from seed since the tree resents being transplanted; they need rich loamy soil. *C. ovata*, the shagbark hickory, has good autumn colour and distinctive rough, peeling bark.

Cercidiphyllum japonicum (above and right) is the treasured Kadsura tree of Japanese gardens. It has a graceful, tiered pagoda-like outline and the shimmering bright yellow autumn foliage will illuminate the garden on a dull day as surely as a 100-watt bulb! All this visual stimulus is augmented by an olfactory one: the fallen leaves, spread in a golden pool beneath the naked boughs, give off a scent of melted chocolate. The finest example I know is at the entrance to the Japanese tea garden in the Blodell Reserve on Bainbridge Island across the Sound from Seattle; even when leafless in the naked depth of winter the tree has a shapely presence. A shrubby relative of the Kadsura, *Disanthus cercidifolius* has redder tints and smaller leaves and is quite rare in cultivation. Both hate lime and need deep, moist acid soil to do their best.

Cercis canadensis 'Forest Pansy' (above), an especially well-coloured cultivar of the common redbud, is much loved by gardeners in the USA, from the mountains of Virginia to the Hill Country of Texas. In the UK and Southern Europe, its counterpart is the Judas tree, *C. siliquastrum*, which William Robinson remarked as having been grown in English gardens for nearly 300 years. Both species have rosy pink flowers on naked branches in the spring, and good autumn colour. They are well-suited to growing in alkaline soils, but will also tolerate acid conditions. They will eventually grow to 9–12m (30–40ft), making broad-crowned trees with spreading branches, but, as Robinson also pointed out, it is the young trees that flower most profusely.

Enkianthus campanulatus (above) is the best of the large to medium-sized shrubs in this genus. The branches are held in loose tiers from which hang the pendulous clusters of tiny, pink-tinted white bell-shaped flowers in early summer. The leaves cluster in whorls around the branches, emphasizing the tiered outline of the shrub. But it is the rich purpling of the foliage in autumn, enhanced by shades of yellow, red and orange, that really makes this shrub outstanding. This species usually gets to roughly 3.5m (12ft), although in ideal conditions of moist acid soil in a woodland setting, it can grow to be much taller.

E. perulatus is about half the size of its sister, but with the same pendent flower clusters and excellent autumn colour. It, too, requires moist acid soil.

E. cernuus f. **rubens** (above) is a red flowered form of the species that grows to a height midway between **E. perulatus** and **E. campanulatus**.

Euonymus alatus, the spindleberry bush, holds its spreading branches like the ribs of a fan, decked out in warm red foliage and hung with dainty clusters of ruby-red fruit. Each berry is shaped like a pendent winged lantern that then splits open to reveal the fleshy coral fruit inside. It's an easy-to-grow shrub for any soil and in sun or part shade. The species has 'winged' bark, vertical striations that stand proud of the surface, giving this deciduous shrub a good texture during winter; the variety **E. a.** var. **apterus** (above), does not have this feature.

Fothergilla major (above) lights up the space beneath the dark branches of *Acer palmatum* 'Ôsakazuki', demonstrating the dynamic effects that can be established with layered planting. Throughout the summer the fothergilla is a rather dull plant, its leaves a dusty grey green. But it compensates by producing scented white bottle-brush flowers on naked stems in spring, while in autumn the leaves are transformed to shades of red, purple, orange and yellow.

Fothergilla species require neutral to acid soils, partial shade and moisture-retentive soil, and so they like to grow in woodland settings or beneath small trees in a garden. *F. major* grows to about 1.8m (6ft) – but very slowly. *F. gardenii* only ever reaches about 1.2m (4ft) and has a mounded habit. The foliage of *F. g.* 'Blue Mist' is prettily tinted a steely blue.

This genus, commonly named witch alder, is part of the Hamamelidaceae family and so is related to witch hazel, the next plant to be described.

Hamamelis mollis (below), the Chinese witch hazel, also bears softly scented flowers in early spring; they resemble little shreds of orange or lemon peel stuck in tight clusters along the naked branches. These large shrubs or small trees grow slowly. However, the wait is worth it, for a mature plant can be 4.5–6m (15–20ft) tall with a broad spreading crown carrying the perfumed flowers well above companion plants and casting a vivid golden autumn spell over the garden. Other witch hazels – all with good autumn colouring – include the cultivars of **H.** × ***intermedia*** with flowers variously coloured coppery-orange ('Jelena'), pale butter-cream yellow ('Pallida') or red ('Ruby Glow') and the cultivar **H. vernalis** 'Sandra' which has purple-flushed young foliage that turns to the best of autumn golds and red. This last plant grows to 3m (10ft), and has a tendency to sucker. Witch hazels prefer neutral to acid soil that is moisture retentive and in part shade.

Hydrangea paniculata (above) is distinguished from the widely popular mophead and lacecap sorts by its plume-like flowerheads, that are conical in shape, rather like out-of-season lilacs coloured white to blushing pink, appearing at the tip of every branch. This hydrangea is widely grown in Japanese gardens. It is an extremely hardy plant and will tolerate even quite warm climates. It can become tall and leggy, but pruning hard back in early spring will control its straggliness as well as encourage plenty of new growth to provide the late-summer flowers, which only appear on the new season's growth. It will grow in sun or part-shade; an avenue lined with this species, weaving through a shady woodland, makes a spectacular show, although even two or three plants add a gentle grace to a mixed group. Also, it will grow on any soil, including chalk.

H. quercifolia (below) is the oak-leaved hydrangea, so-called for the shape of its leaves which colour well in autumn, in shades of purple and russet red on peeling cinnamon-bark stems. These rich tints perfectly complement the white flower-heads, which are similar in shape to those of *H. paniculata* but rather more lumpen. It also has a lax, sprawling 'picturesque' habit. Grow it in rich, moisture-retentive soil in part shade; it is not entirely hardy, and does its very best in warm gardens, so otherwise give it shelter.

Ilex (above) is one of the most useful shrubs a gardener can grow; as William Robinson wrote, 'As regards the uses of the Holly, they are so many in the garden that it is difficult even to generalise them. As shelter in bold groups, dividing lines, hedges, beautiful effects of fruit in autumn, masses of evergreen foliage, bright glistening colour from variegated kinds… every kind of delightful use may be found for them in gardens.'

The light-reflecting quality of its glossy evergreen leaves is part of holly's great charm, adding depth to a mixed group of deciduous and evergreen shrubs. The berries also bring colour to the autumn garden and, depending on the species, range from bright yellow to ruby red. There is also a daunting selection of leaf shapes, texture, variegation and colour to choose from. Among the most popular variegated sorts of the common English holly, *I. aquifolium*, are: 'Argentea

Marginata', 'Silver Queen' and 'Handsworth New Silver', all with white variegation; 'Golden Milkboy' and 'Golden Queen' have yellow variegation. *I. a.* 'Green Pillar' is solidly green and sturdily erect while 'Myrtifolia' has small green leaves. Some hollies have a distinct blue cast to the leaves, especially *I.* × *meserveae* Blue Angel, Blue Prince and Blue Princess. *I. aquifolium* 'Ferox' is the hedgehog holly, so called for the spine-covered surface of the leaves.

I. × *altaclerensis* is natural, tall-growing, robust garden hybrid that has a pleasing pyramidal shape and is nearly thornless. One of the most popular cultivars is 'Lawsoniana', with strong yellow splashes on the leaves. *I.* × *a* 'Golden King' is also widely grown, and despite its name, is a female plant. This is important to note when making a selection, since to have berries it is essential to grow both male and female plants.

Nyssa sylvatica (below) is the tupelo or black gum tree of the east and southern USA, but it is fairly hardy and will grow in moist ground quite happily. It makes a huge tree, up to 30m (100ft) tall, so it really needs plenty of room to show off its elegant pyramidal shape. The young foliage is bright green and throughout summer it holds a glossy gleam, turning in autumn to all the shades of a harvest sunset. Like *Liquidambar*, this is one of the best specimen trees for an autumn garden, best suited to acid soils.

Parrotia persica (above), the Persian ironwood, is another splendid specimen for the autumn garden. It has an elegant habit, growing slowly to make a medium-sized tree of about 9m (30ft) in height, usually with several trunks supporting a broad horizontal spreading crown. The foliage is a dull green colour in summer but during autumn the downward curving leaves turn from yellow through dark red to purple. This tree does well on moisture-retentive, neutral to chalky soils, in a sunny or partly shaded position. It is a relative of the witch hazel.

Parthenocissus tricuspidata (left) is the variously hated or loved Boston ivy; hated because it is said to destroy walls by its self-clinging habit of climbing, using little suckering rootlets to attach itself to the mortar (while others claim that the leaves protect the brickwork from the elements). It is loved for the brightness of its autumn colour, and there is no question that it and its relative, *P. quinquefolia*, or Virginia creeper, epitomize autumn colouring. But both should be used sparingly: Gertrude Jekyll made the valid point that climbers should not be allowed to completely disguise the architecture which supports them (unless of course that was the whole point of planting them in the first place). *Parthenocissus* will grow anywhere if the soil is well-drained.

Polystichum setiferum (above) is a common woodland fern in both Northern Europe and North America where it grows easily in the light cool shade and moist, humus-rich soil of the forest floor and woodland edge. There are many other species and some cultivars that have distinctly curious leaf formations, like *P. s.* 'Densum Erectum' which I can only describe as having leaves that are fully double, so it looks like an especially fluffy plume of feathers. The habits of most of these ferns when young makes them resemble shuttlecocks, and the upright growing fronds look exceptionally pretty waving over bright coloured groundcover or beneath the shade of an autumn-tinted shrub, like the red-tinted leaves of *Viburnum plicatum* shown here.

Prunus species and cultivars are many and all have something worth writing about, but for autumn colour, the ornamental cherry species, *P. sargentii* (above), remains my favourite. A young tree planted in moist but well-drained soil in sun or part shade, will quickly make a medium-sized tree up to 7.5m (25ft) tall. The tree has an upward spreading outline, like a funnel or martini glass, and the pendulous clusters of pale pinky white flowers appear in early spring followed closely by the copper-tinted juvenile leaves – very elegant. In autumn the leaves cling on and, in my garden at least, seemed to change overnight from green to flaming tones of yellow, red and orange. Then, just as sud-

denly, they seemed to drop, making a pool of sunbeams on the dewy autumn grass – very dramatic. So with all this theatre, it is one tree I do not hesitate to recommend for the small garden.

P. serrula (above) is another cherry worth having, but for its bark rather than

its visual bite (pun entirely intended!). The sheen and warm glow of the peeling rust-red bark is this tree's main claim to garden space, although it does have a pretty spreading habit and pleasing white flowers in spring. The bark is good all year round, so call this another winner.

P. 'Shirotae' (above) is typical of many of the ornamental cherries in having good autumn colour. It, too, is a medium-sized tree, and the spring flower show is composed of quite large, single white blossoms in pendent clusters. But the best for single flowers and with good autumn colour is the great white cherry, *P.* 'Taihaku'.

Quercus rubra (left), or red oak, along with the sugar maple, is one of the main players in the New England autumn colour cast. Similarly, it lights up many an English landscape, but without perhaps the vivacity it displays in America. In Texas, too, the red oak is a favourite autumn tree and its bright red thumbprint can be easily spotted amongst the dull green crowns of the evergreen live oaks (*Q. virginiana*) that cloak the Hill Country.

Oaks grow slowly to make large statuesque trees, which is what makes their wood so dense and valuable, and will grow in most soils in sun or part shade. *Q. coccinea*, the scarlet oak, however, makes a relatively fast-growing, medium-sized tree and has good red colouring – some would say the best of all.

Viburnum sargentii (above) displays its bright red, glossy berries against soft gold foliage; *V. s.* 'Onondaga' is more dramatically coloured, however. The cultivar has a more upright habit than the species and the young foliage is coloured soft purple-green in spring, and deepens to a dusky maroon in autumn. The flower umbels are small and white, shining out amidst the dark leaves. This is a good plant for a sombre corner in shade and moisture-retentive soil.

Rhus typhina (above), the staghorn sumach, makes a spectacular display in autumn with its brillant red, compound leaves, gracefully displayed on spreading branches. Each leaflet of the cultivar *R. t.* 'Dissecta' is deeply toothed, giving this shrub a much lacier appearence, although still with the same flaming colour. This shrub takes its common name from the fuzzy texture of the new shoots in spring which recall the down on the antlers of a young stag. The flowers, too (right), are enjoyed for their curious velvety texture. Sumach is a relative of the other brilliant autumn show-off, *Cotinus coggygria*, or smoke tree, with its self-descriptively named cultivars such as 'Royal Purple', 'Pink Champagne' and 'Flame'.

These colourful shrubs will grow in any soil in sun or part shade; sumach has a tendency to sucker, but it is easily controlled by pulling out young upstarts.

Vitis is the grape genus, which includes some very autumnally attractive species, as well as the delicious sorts used for making wine. For breath-taking foliage, size-wise and colour-wise, *V. coignetiae* (above and right), is hard to beat. Above, it is happily mixed with *Clematis orientalis*, whose wispy seedheads provide an interesting textural contrast with the vine's large leaves. *V. coignetiae* is a hardy, rampant grower, once established, and can be cut down to the knuckle each spring, or back to a trained framework of main branches, from where it will throw long wands that are soon covered in huge, heart-shaped leaves. These are deeply veined and rough in texture, and in the autumn turn the best shades of red and purple. But it really does need room to spread – in my English garden it consumed the garage, but then I never was much on judicious pruning, preferring to see things romp away. I've also grown *V. vinifera* 'Purpurea' with its dark purple leaves and fruit, and *V.* 'Brant', another decorative variety, which is mentioned in Chapter 4. Of all the grape vines in cultivation, to date these three are the only ones that have been given the Award of Garden Merit by the Royal Horticultural Society. Well-drained soil in a sunny position is what suits them best.

GRASSES

Once under-appreciated, ornamental grasses, bamboos and forbs in general are enjoying their new-found stardom; from Munich to Seattle the graceful blades and twitching seedheads are very much in vogue as the main ingredient in 'natural', 'wild', 'ecological' and 'new perennial' – call it what you will – gardens. This makes sense, of course, when you observe that much of nature's planting is woven into a grass matrix.

Cortaderia selloana 'Sunningdale Silver' (previous page) is one of the most widely grown of those South American natives, the fabulous pampas grasses. The cultivar and the species, *C. selloana* (above left), have towering, ultra-fluffy plumes but there are smaller growing varieties, such as *C. s.* 'Pumila', which is good in small gardens, and the gold-variegated *C. s.* 'Aureolineata' with yellow stripes running down each leaf blade.

Forming huge clumps, pampas grass begins to flower in late summer carrying the erect stems – up to 2.7m (9ft) tall – throughout the autumn and winter. By the end of the season, the plumes look pretty shabby and so should be cut down.

Plant in the spring in deep, sandy, well-drained soil in a sheltered spot out of cold winds for the best results.

Hordeum jubatum (above), the squirrel or fox-tail barley grass, is a short-lived perennial that is most generally grown as an annual. It is usually cultivated for its fine seedheads, which dry well for decorations, and less often, simply because it is such a good mingler in the garden. It does best in dry soil – too much moisture makes it 'fat' and the plumes are less likely to survive cutting and drying well.

Hakonechloa macra 'Aureola' (left) is a grass much used in Japanese gardens, probably because of its waterfall-like spray of golden variegated foliage that moves langourously when stirred by the breeze. It does best in a sheltered, partly shaded site, although in cool climates it can be put in the sun where it will colour up well with a reddish blush.

Miscanthus, or maiden grass, is in my estimation the grass genus *par excellence*. The foliage is varied and refined, the flower plumes delicately tinted and with a silken sheen. The flowers appear late in the summer and carry on well through autumn and winter. There is also a good selection of size and height from which to choose.

Don't cram the plants into borders, but give them space to breathe so that their graceful form is displayed without hindrance – *Miscanthus* is definitely an 'architectural' plant.

M. sinensis is the species most often grown in gardens and there are numerous cultivars ranging in height from 1.2m (4ft) (*M. s.* 'Kleine Silberspinne') to 2.1m (7ft) (*M. s.* 'Grosse Fontäne'). *M. s.* 'Zebrinus' (above) is a popular variety that is notable for the yellow variegation that runs across each leaf blade, while *M. s.* 'Malepartus' (left), has the most pronounced red autumn colouring of the genus.

The feathery plumes of all *Miscanthus* are a good feature, and they do have a strong visual and tactile quality thanks to

clump-forming grasses in conjunction with other forbs and perennials. In this small section of Mark Brown's *Miscanthus* border he has used, reading from foreground to back, the grass *Deschampsia cespitosa* 'Goldtau', white-flowered *Sedum spectabile* 'Stardust', *M. sinensis* 'Ferne Osten', the common herb fennel (*Foeniculum vulgare*), *M. s.* 'Rotsilber' and *M. s.* 'Ernst Pagels'. Incidentally, *Deschampsia*, or tufted hair grass, is another gorgeous autumn-flowering grass, with long loose flower panicles of extreme delicacy that dry from soft wine red to bright biscuit brown. In contrast, the leaves are long, spiky in texture and dark glossy green. It will seed freely.

Molinia caerulea ssp. *caerulea* 'Variegata' (above) is the variegated form of purple moor grass, a clumping perennial that is native to acid heathland. This white-variegated form is the one most often found in gardens, thanks to the white stripe that runs the length of each leaf accentuating the graceful curve and movement of the foliage. The erect flower stems turn burnished gold in autumn and stand well above the leaves. Its relative, *M. c.* ssp. *arundinacea* is another bundle of golden autumn colour, with stiff flower stems and tidy clumping foliage. These grasses are generally small growing, typically only 1–1.2m (3–4ft), and ideal for heavy, acid, moisture-retentive soil.

their soft glossy texture that catches the sunlight and the eye. *M.* 'Silberfeder' (above), which translates as 'Silver Feather', earned its name for just these reasons.

Miscanthus will grow in most soils, but really does its best in deeply dug, humus-rich soil that is well-drained but not dry. The spent flower spikes and foliage can be cut down to a height of about 25–30cm (10–12in) in the spring, and the plants then mulched with well-rotted compost. Plants can also be lifted, divided and replanted in the spring.

A mixed border of *Miscanthus* (right), shows what can be done with these

Stipa is the genus that provides the other 'must grow' grasses, and I have tried the three shown here and will happily do so again. Nothing quite captures the eye like *S. gigantea* (above), with its golden-awned seed spikes waving in the breeze above the delicately leaved tussocks of dusky green foliage. It's a sight to make you stand still and contemplate – something one should find frequent occasion to do in a garden. From flower tip to leaf toe, this grass is about 1.8m (6ft) tall; don't crowd it, but do use it as a signpost plant or to give particular emphasis to a specific garden area, and make sure the sunlight can catch the seedheads in autumn. The only trouble is that the stems are quite pliant and a stiff breeze can knock them to the ground and end the show, so select a sheltered but sunny corner.

Similarly but on a less grand scale, *S. tenuissima* (right), the angel hair grass, has stunning seedheads, like trailing threads of spun silver, seen here spilling over the frosted grey-green foliage rosettes of *Phlomis samia*. This is the sort of contrast that is attainable with ornamental grasses; playing broad leaf against narrow

leaf to create varied textures and shadow. I have found that this particular *Stipa* grows easily from seed; simply pull the threads from the seedheads and lay them in a tray of moist compost. Cover them with a sifting of soil, or else spread them thinly in a prepared seedbed and cover lightly. Keep well watered until germination and there will soon be lots of little bright green shaving brushes ready to plant out in the garden. This grass works especially well with members of the Compositae family like *Anthemis*.

Stipa calamagrostis (above) is one of the most free-flowering of all the grasses, with the fluffy plumes appearing in mid-summer and carrying right through autumn and winter. It is so dependable, it can almost be boring, except for its grace and winning ways as a flower for drying. Massed plantings of this *Stipa*, as seen here with *Sedum* 'Strawberries and Cream', are most effective. One other *Stipa* to be sure to grow is *S. arundinacea* because of its graceful waterfall of foliage that takes on a rusty orange glow in autumn.

All that these grasses require is a sunny spot and well-drained soil that doesn't dry out totally. I don't recommend cutting them down ever, but rake through the foliage with your fingers during the early spring to remove the spent flowerheads and any dead foliage.

BERRIES

Summer flowers give way to seed-bearing, autumn fruit as part of the regenerative process of nature. Gardens benefit from this with the ornamental riches of many varieties of brightly coloured, curiously formed, glistening or differently textured berries and seed-containing pods.

Berries are *indehiscent*, which means that they do not open to disperse their cache of seed, as a *dehiscent* pod would do. A berry, instead, contains the seed in a protective shell. The seed is not dispersed until the shell rots away or is digested by an animal; berry-eating birds are among the best seed-scatterers in nature!

Some dehiscent plants have especially attractive pods or bracts, like *Amicia zygomeris* (previous page), a member of the pea family, Leguminosae, from the woodlands of western Mexico. The butterfly-like purple-stained wings at the leaf axils make this a most unusual autumn ornamental. The top growth will not withstand frost, but it will shoot again from the roots if protected by mulch.

Arum maculatum, also known as lords-and-ladies, Johnny-jump-up, and cuckoo-pint is a hedgerow plant. Its large spade-shaped leaves appear in spring and are followed by an erect, hooded flower spathe that gives way to a spike of orange to crimson berries, similar to the spike of *A. italicum* ssp. *italicum* 'Marmoratum' (above). The flare of red against the soft grey leaves of *Stachys byzantina* 'Cotton Boll' is as fine an autumn feature as you could care to have, but earlier in the year, the silvery veins of the arum's foliage blend well with the ever-grey of the lamb's ears. Arums generally prefer deep moist soil, but I have grown just this combination in free-draining, sandy soil and really enjoyed the seasonal show.

Berberis is a large genus of evergreen, semi-evergreen and deciduous shrubs that are extremely popular for their pretty flower clusters. Some also have attractive foliage, like **B. thunbergii,** which has pale green foliage that turns bright orange in autumn, and the purple-leaved **B. t.** f. *atropurpurea.* This particular barberry is a small shrub and can be used to make a clipped hedge, the dwarf **B. t.** 'Atropurpurea Nana' can be used for a low knot-garden edging.

Generally, barberries have blue-black berries, but there are few that have all the attractive flower and foliage features, as well as colourful autumn fruit. **B. prattii** (above) is one to grow for attractive berries; these are long-lasting and daintily coloured porcelain-white before turning to blush pink. **B.** × *ottawensis* 'Superba' has good purple foliage and yellow flowers which are followed by red berries. **B. wilsoniae** makes a dense mound of blue-green foliage that takes on good autumn colour accented by its coral-red berries.

Callicarpa bodinieri var. *giraldii* (above) is one of the few shrubs that can provide such a striking fuchsia-pink berry colour. It is small-growing and makes a rounded deciduous shrub with bronze-tinged juvenile foliage and clusters of pale lilac flowers along the stems in midsummer. It is best to plant several shrubs together in a small group to ensure cross-pollination and so have plenty of fruit. It is quite hardy and will grow in well-drained soil in a partly shaded spot. Look for the form *C. b.* var. *g.* 'Profusion'; so named for the abundance of its colourful berries.

C. japonica is a small shrub with a compact habit of growth; the cultivar *C. j.* 'Leucocarpa' has white fruit.

Prune the shrubs hard in spring, cutting out old wood to the ground to make way for the prolifically produced new shoots. The berry-laden branches are especially popular with flower arrangers.

Cotoneaster is probably the most popular of autumn-berry shrubs and particularly for wall-training, as its stiff branches can be espaliered, cordon-trained, and generally pruned and manipulated to any linear pattern you care to create. Or they can simply be left to find their own form. Among the most widely used is the fishbone cotoneaster, *C. horizontalis*, because its natural habit is to spread its branches like the ribs of a fish. *C. microphyllus* carries the leaves in tight clusters close to the stem with its bright red berries studded amongst the greenery like jewels. *C. × suecicus* 'Coral Beauty' (above) has glossy green leaves to show off the bright red berries. *C. frigidus* 'Cornubia' has a brilliant abundance of coral-red fruit decorating each exceedingly tall arching branch. *C. × watereri* 'Pink Champagne' has yellow berries that blush pink as they age. *C. bullatus* has particularly large oval leaves and is another tall-growing shrub, to at least 2.7m (9ft). They will grow anywhere in well-drained soil.

Euonymus latifolius (below) is a curiously coloured tree and relative of the spindle-berry, *E. alatus*, with pendent lantern-shaped berries in early autumn amidst the red-tinted acid-green foliage. There is a fuchsia-pink fleshy cup surrounding the orange berry – an outstanding combination, but it is not a plant often seen in gardens. In good rich soil it will make a medium-sized tree, to about 6m (20ft), with a broad spreading crown.

Gaultheria, once more commonly known as *Pernettya*, is an outstanding evergreen shrub that carries clusters of brightly coloured berries, in a wide range of colours, throughout autumn. They are especially valued by florists and flower arrangers for their quite formal berry sprays. *G. mucronata* is a small-leaved shrub with many named hybrids that positively groan under their burden of autumn fruit. But this will only happen if a male plant is located with a group of female plants, so be sure to get both sexes. They require cool, moist, acid soil and sun or part shade.

Hybrids include *G. m.* 'Mascula' (above), *G. m.* 'Crimsonia', *G. m.* 'Mulberry Wine' with magenta berries, the lilac pink *G. m.* 'Pink Pearl', *G. m.* 'White Pearl', and the pale pink *G. m.* 'Sea Shell'.

Hypericum androsaemum (above), a native British plant commonly known as tutsan, is one of the St John's worts and is a small deciduous shrub that flowers from early summer through autumn. The flowers are small and bright yellow and the soft green leaves are comparatively large and oval. Like most hypericums, the stems are flushed with red, but the most striking aspect is the berries; surrounded by star-like sepals they turn from rusty red to glittering black beads. This hypericum will often continue in flower even as it goes to seed, so you get a pretty mix of yellow petals and clusters of tinted berries. It's not too fussy about the soil it's planted in or its position.

Hippophae rhamnoides (above) is commonly called sea buckthorn since it is one of the best plants for seaside gardens. The colouring is superb, however, in any garden, with the narrow, silvery foliage perfectly complementing the warm terracotta-orange berries that crowd the stems in autumn. Berries will be borne only if male and female shrubs are planted together to allow for cross-pollination. It is a large, thorny shrub, resistant to drought, that will reach 6m (20ft) and sucker freely, eventually making a dense thicket of sharp spiny branches.

In May, the crab apple trees in the hedgerows around my English garden burst into flower, which was always the signal to begin planning which flavour of herb jellies to make that autumn; the tart little green fruit of *Malus sylvestris* making the most delicious base for all sorts of sweet condiments. Ornamentally it was not up to much, but there are many other crab apples that will decorate the autumn garden, like *M.* 'John Downie', with edible crimson-red fruit, or *M.* × *zumi* 'Golden Hornet' (right), a small spreading tree with drooping branches covered in small yellow apples. *M. hupehensis* is a good ornamental crab apple covered in a profusion of scented white flowers in spring followed by red-flushed yellow fruit in autumn.

Physalis alkekengi (above), or Chinese lantern, is a long-time cottage garden and flower arranger's favourite perennial. The bright papery shells surrounding the glossy orange fruit are what make it so attractive, from early summer right through autumn. During winter the shell will gradually disintegrate, leaving only the veins and exposing the fruit within a wiry skeleton cage. Its relative, *P. peruviana*, is the 'designer' fruit known as the Cape gooseberry, the darling of gourmet chefs who peel back the outer papery wrapping to expose the orange fruit, which is then used to decorate finished dishes. The garden perennial, which is occasionally treated as an annual, is a moderately fast colonizer and looks well among late-flowering summer borders where the sharp orange tints make a good feature. Plant it in any well-drained soil, choosing a position in part shade to full sun. It will withstand a fair amount of neglect which is why it is so often found in derelict garden sites.

Phytolacca americana (above), or pokeweed, is a native American perennial sometimes known as red-ink plant, since the berry juice was once used as a writing material. Long ago, the juice was also used to deepen the colour of port wine – a practice long discontinued since it did nothing for the flavour, and it was later discovered, over time, that the berries have a toxic effect. Pokeweed root is an important medicinal herb, and the young shoots emerging in late spring were said to be a good substitute for asparagus. In the garden it is an oddity, which is why I included it; tall-growing, weird perennials can spice up the action, and the pokeweed's rose-madder stems and blackberry-blue berries are truly eye-catching. It needs moist soil to do well, in shade or sun.

Pyracantha, or firethorn, is a fairly large group of evergreen shrubs that are often grown like cotoneaster, as climbers and as wall-cover. In spring, clusters of tiny white flowers shroud the thorny branches. These are followed in autumn by clusters of berries in shades of red, orange or yellow that persist until the birds have eaten them all, if it is a lean winter, or throughout winter, if there is plenty of other food around. *P.* 'Orange Glow' (above) is the most widely used orange-berried sort, while *P. rogersiana* 'Flava' is noted for its abundant yellow berries. *P.* 'Watereri' has glossy green leaves, a compact habit and plenty of red berries.

The plants do best in a sheltered spot in sun or part shade. To train against a wall, tie in leaders to a wire support during the first few years, then cut back the long lateral growth produced after flowering.

Rosa species and hybrids include many that produce attractive hips; probably the best known are those of *R. rugosa*, which are exceedingly round, almost bulbous, bright red and shiny. But there are several roses that produce curiously coloured hips and standing out among these are the hips of *R.* 'Geranium' (right), and *R. glauca* (above). The latter is an especially good rose with faded raspberry-pink single flowers, blue-grey foliage and pretty brick-red hips. *R.* 'Geranium' has foliage that is quite lacy in appearance and the little hips are like orange confetti scattered across the branches. *R. pimpinellifolia* makes a thicket of spiny branches covered in tiny

leaves and soft pink, double flowers followed by glossy black hips, while *R. nitida* has orange hips and scarlet foliage in autumn.

Species roses need room to spread out but work better in borders than hybrid teas or floribundas. Well-drained soil in a sunny spot suits best, and the only pruning needed is a tidy up in early spring to remove crowded stems and old worn-out wood.

Sorbus, or mountain ash, is a widely varied genus that includes numerous small trees that have good autumn foliage, clusters of colourful fruit, or both features. One such is *S. commixta* 'Embley' (right), that has fine green foliage that colours to rusty red in late autumn, and heavy clusters of bright red fruit. *S. vilmorinii* (below) has pendent clusters of red fruit that fade to a pale pink colour or to white tinted with rose-red, amidst dark red autumn foliage.

S. hupehensis is an erect young tree, gradually spreading with age, that has fine blue-green foliage and loose panicles of faded pink berries. The one other notable characteristic is that the flower clusters often smell quite nasty; I grew *S. hupehensis* for the berries, but in early summer wondered where the smell of fetid meat was coming from – not very nice. So plant well away from open windows or any areas where you sit out in the garden.

FLOWERS

Every season has its 'colour scheme': spring has shades of pastel blue and yellow with hints of pink; summer's palette is warmed with by the passage of the days and the addition of red and orange, until we reach autumn, when saturated colours begin to appear. Because of the deepening shadows and darkening foliage, the flower colours stand out all the more. Now is not the time to start putting the garden to bed for the winter, it is an occasion to celebrate the finely painted scene that nature lays out for us and from which we can draw inspiration for next year's garden glory.

Monkshood, *Aconitum carmichaelii* 'Arendsii' (left), is typical of the flower colour found in autumn gardens. It is quite possibly the most intensely blue perennial, bearing the spikes of bell-shaped flowers on sturdy erect spikes. It does best in well-drained soil in part shade. Weave beneath and between autumn-colouring shrubs.

Allium tuberosum (above), with white-flowers, and the purple *A. senescens* ssp. *montanum* (below), are among the late-flowering species in the popular ornamental section of the onion genus. These erect-stemmed bulbous plants look great with grasses and do best in free-draining soil, in full sun. They increase rapidly so lift and replant the bulblets frequently. Both of these only reach about 45cm (18in) so use them near the front of borders or among groundcovering plants so that their flowers are shown off to best advantage.

Anemone × *hybrida* 'Honorine Jobert' (below) is one of the finest autumn-flowering perennials. These anemones are commonly called Japanese windflowers, and they do have a graceful movement in the soft cool breezes of the season. The erect wiry stems carry the flowers well above

the palmate foliage and a single plant will spread steadily to make a sizeable clump. As the young leaves unfurl in late summer they have a silky filamented surface, so the plant is good looking for most of its time in the garden. They do best in moisture-retentive soil in full sun or part shade. *A.* × *h.* 'Max Vogel' has rosy pink, semi-double flowers and *A. hupehensis* var. *japonica* 'Prinz Heinrich' has single pink ones. Mix them up for an informal planting among pink and white autumn-berried shrubs.

Aster, the Michaelmas daisy, is probably the ultimate autumn perennial flower; at this time of year few other plants can compete with the range of colour, height and flower size found in this genus, as can be plainly seen in the nursery rows at Waterperry gardens (above). Dan Hinkley, proprietor of Heronswood Nursery, Washington, has written most eloquently about the true value of asters, 'When the leaves have crisped on the Golden Hops, the grasses have splayed and even the fruiting plants have lost their luster, it is the asters that bring clarity to the season and reason to continue with garden strolls in the evening.' There are two species from which the various named cultivars are taken; *A. novae-angliae* and *A. novi-belgii*. The first are much more vigorous and disease resistant, while the second are prone to mildew attacks that corrupt the foliage and weaken the plant and so must be regularly sprayed. Then there are the species which offer the gardener a limited range of colour but a huge selection for height, from the ground-hugging 15cm (6in) tall *A. dumosus* to the towering *A. umbellatus* at nearly 1.8m (6ft). Generally hardy plants, they require little attention and prefer well-drained good soil in sun or part shade. The plants benefit from mulching to keep the roots moist in dry spells.

A. cordifolius 'Aldebaran' (left) makes a loose open plant with clusters of lilac-white flowers. *A. divaricatus* (above) has

tiny star-like flowers on open wiry branches. *A.* × *frikartii* 'Mönch' (above) makes sturdy clumps about 45cm (18in) high. *A. novi-belgii* 'Saint Egwyn' (below) is pink-flowered and *A. amellus* 'Veilchenkönigin' (right) is typical of the rich colouring found among Michaelmas daisies; this sort makes healthy clump-forming plants about 30–40cm (12–18in) tall.

Bupleurum fruticosum (above) is an evergreen perennial that makes quite a sizable mound of blue-green foliage topped by umbells of brassy yellow flowers. It does well in gardens near the sea, and likes a well-drained soil in full sun. A much finer plant is *B. falcatum* which grows to only about 30cm (1ft) tall and has lacy umbels of tiny yellow flowers. It has a pleasant habit of self-seeding itself through grasses and among annual flowers.

Caryopteris × *clandonensis* 'Arthur Simmonds' (above) is a small deciduous shrub that is invaluable for the fine blue flowers it carries along the length of its wand-like branches. It does best if cut back hard each spring to promote new shoots and it likes well-drained soil in full sun. The leaves of *C.* × *c.* 'Worcester Gold' (left) have a pale yellow cast that perfectly sets off the light blue of the flowers.

Choisya ternata (above), the Mexican orange blossom, is a glossy leafed, ever-green shrub that carries highly fragrant white flowers in late summer through autumn. Often the flowering tips of the branches can be damaged by frost, but just cut away the scorched leaves and it will soon reshoot. It does well in any well-drained but moisture-retentive soil, in sun or part shade.

Chrysanthemum 'Belle', with red flowers, yellow-flowered *C.* 'Honey' (left) and brick-red *C.* 'Louise' (above) are good examples of the late-flowering border chrysanthe-mums. Along with Michaelmas daisies, these are among the showiest of autumn-flowering perennials, and will flower dependably even if totally neglected, as I know, having been a very lax chrysanthe-mum grower! They are excellent cut flow-ers and easy to care for in the garden, requiring well-drained soil and full sun.

Cleome hassleriana (above) is commonly called the spider flower. It is a showy half-hardy annual that quickly grows from an early-spring sowing, made when all chance of frost is past, to eventually reach at least 1.2m (4ft) in height. The flowers are scented and top each stiffly erect stem with blooms in shades of pink, white and mauve. It makes a good show in mixed borders and among shrubs, liking well-drained but moisture-retentive soil in part shade or sun.

Clerodendrum bungei (above) is a tall-growing (to at least 2.4m (8ft)) shrub that has broad, dark green leaves and umbels of flowers that are red in bud fading to lilac-pink – quite a vivid show. The stems are dark and stiffly erect and the shrub suckers quite freely, so will in time form a dense thicket. Frost can cut it down, but it will soon shoot again. Watch out for the leaves, which smell badly when crushed. Plant in any soil, in sun or part shade.

Colchicum autumnale (left), *C. speciosum* (above) and *C. bivonae* (right) are all hardy autumn-flowering plants that grow from corms planted in the spring. The flowers are sometimes called naked ladies because the leaves do not appear until after the flowers have faded, making large clumps of broad, strap-like, bright green foliage that endure for most of the winter and well into spring. The several flowers appear from each corm.

Colchicums do best planted in an open sunny position and well-drained soil. They work well among deciduous shrubs or naturalized in tall grass that is only cut during late summer.

Crinum × ***powellii*** (above) is a tall-growing bulbous perennial that has drooping trumpet-shaped flowers atop thick stems; the flowers are scented and, like colchicums, appear before the foliage. Crinums are not completely hardy, so plant in a sunny, sheltered spot in deeply dug, rich soil that is well-drained but does not dry out.

Crocosmia × ***crocosmiiflora*** 'Star of the East' (above) is a clump-forming perennial with superior late-summer to early-autumn flowers. This variety has glowing bright orange flowers, but there are other species and cultivars that take on colours from yellow (***C.*** × ***c.*** 'Citronella') to deep crimson (***C.*** 'Lucifer'). ***C.*** × ***c.*** 'Emily Mackenzie' is popular for its wide-open flowers, where most other crocosmias have rather closed tubular blossoms. ***C.*** × ***c.*** 'Solfaterre' has warm apricot-coloured flowers and the foliage is flushed with warm brown; it looks quite striking when grown with ***Stipa arundinacea***. These plants grow from corms and gradually increase to form sizeable clumps. They like full sun and well-drained soil.

Cyclamen hederifolium (above) is a hardy cyclamen that grows wild in the woods and meadows of the sunny Mediterranean countries. It grows from corms and can be easily increased from seed sown fresh in late autumn or as soon as it ripens. As the flowers fade, the stem curls up, drawing the seed capsule down to corm level; when the capsule ripens, the coil springs out, shooting the seed all round. The trick is to catch the pod just before this happens and release the sticky little seeds into some good sandy compost. Plant corms just below the soil surface in full sun or part shade, in well-drained soil.

Dahlia is a genus that offers a huge array of highly colourful flowers in all sorts of shapes and sizes, from tight little pompons to great spidery objects like *D.* 'Reputation' (above), and they are divided into groups according to the type of flower they have: single, water-lily, collerette, cactus and so on. Dahlias are tender perennials that grow from tubers which are generally lifted after flowering and overwintered with protection from frost; a dusting with fungicide protects the resting tubers from botrytis. In spring, the tubers begin to shoot and plants can then be increased by removing the shoots and rooting them in trays of compost. Dahlias require a good well-dug soil, that is well-drained but does not dry out. Plant them in a sunny spot. Tall-growing varieties will need staking.

Eucomis bicolor (above), the pineapple flower, is an exotic-looking bulbous plant that is hardy if given a thick mulch blanket in winter. I have grown these in containers and enjoyed the fleshy seedpods that array themselves along the flower spike as much as the starry little flowers. In fact, *Eucomis* seeded itself into the paving cracks beneath the pots, so it must be quite robust. Put three or four bulbs into large urns or tubs for best effect. They like full sun and well-drained soil.

Euphorbia seguieriana (above) is a showy perennial about 45cm (18in) tall, with acid green, terminal flower clusters in spring that turn to bright green buttons atop autumn-coloured stems. Another euphorbia that gives good autumn value is the clump-forming *E. nicaeensis*; the foliage is a cool blue-grey, the flowers and pods more yellow than green and the stems turn bright red in autumn. Dark red, tinged with green is the predominant year-round colour of *E. dulcis* 'Chameleon'; it seeds freely and spreads by underground stems. These plants prefer well-drained soil in full sun.

Fuchsia flowers are one of autumn's great delights; there are all sorts of combinations of the red, pink, purple and white colouring and of the sizes of flower – from frou-frou doubles as full as a ballerina's skirts, to skeletal singles with needle-narrow petals, and all with a graceful pendent habit. Combine this with bright foliage, as in *F. magellanica* 'Versicolor' (above), and the plant becomes a double-feature winner in the autumn garden. Fuchsias do well in full sun or part shade and well-drained soil that does not dry out.

Gentiana 'Strathmore' (above) is one of the finest blue-flowered plants in the garden, no matter what the season. The huge blue trumpets nestle neatly into the narrow, dark green glossy foliage in a most comfortable manner, making a vibrant carpet in a rockery or raised bed. Gentians need neutral to acid soils that are rich in humus or well-rotted compost and which never dry out. *G. sino-ornata* is another autumn-flowering gentian that carries white-throated, azure-blue flowers atop rosettes of grassy foliage. It does especially well in acid soil near a water feature since it likes a moist atmosphere.

Helenium 'Bruno' (above) is one of several sneezeweed cultivars that contribute sturdy daisy-like flowers to the autumn border. This is a bushy perennial about 60–100cm (2–3ft) in height, with sprays of dusky red flowers in late summer through autumn. It does best in well-drained soil in full sun.

Helianthus 'Capenoch Star' (below) is a perennial relative of the annual sunflower, *H. annuus*, and makes a branching, tall-growing plant to about 1.2m (4ft), with lemon-yellow flowers at the end of each stem. The perennial sunflowers can be invasive, so allow plenty of space, although regular lifting and dividing will go some way towards keeping them in check. The willow-leafed sunflower, *H. salicifolius*, is particularly invasive, and is also nearly 2.1m (7ft) tall when growing in the right conditions of sun and well-drained soil. But for a colourful autumn screen of bright sunny flowers it is hard to beat.

Hedera helix (above), or common ivy, might not seem like a first choice for inclusion among colourful autumn flowers, but the balls of bright green blooms against the glossy malachite of the evergreen foliage are really quite striking. These eventually turn to little black berries and constitute a feature that often goes unnoticed. It pays to be aware of all the attributes a plant possesses, not just the most obvious ones; you never know what you will discover and be able to use to good effect in a plant grouping.

Impatiens tinctoria (above) is a native of the moist mountain forests of northern Africa, so is only perennial in mild climates and with protection. The flowers are large and orchid-like and the broad oval leaves dark green. It will do well in deep, rich, moist soil and looks especially pretty naturalized among trees or tall-growing shrubs. The other *Impatiens* that is fun to grow is the white-flowered form of the Peruvian balsam, *I. glandulifera* 'Candida' – as long as you do not let it get out of hand. It seeds freely, so take care, but the tall, up to 1.8m (6ft), stems of pure white flowers really are eye-catching if left to colonize at the edge of woodland.

Leonotis leonurus (above), or lion's ear, is a semi-evergreen shrub, up to 1.2m (4ft) tall, with loose open branches and whorls of bright orange, slightly felted flowers. It is not fully hardy, so does best with a sunny, sheltered position in well-drained soil – moisture sitting around the base of the plant will cause it to rot. It looks rather nifty mixed up with the tall stems and purple flowers of *Verbena bonariensis*.

Leycesteria formosa (right), or Himalayan honeysuckle, has its place in the autumn garden because of its curiously laid-back pendent blooms that are dark purple bracts tipped by tiny white true flowers. It should be cut to the ground in spring and will quickly send up new stems, to 1.5m (5ft) tall. It does well in sun or part shade and well-drained soil, and makes a good quick screening plant.

Liriope muscari (above), or lily turf, is a groundcovering evergreen, making spreading clumps of long narrow dark green leaves, from which emerge spikes of lavender-purple flowers in late summer. The plants spread by underground rhizomes and do well in dry freely-draining soil in sun or part shade. Only about 30cm (1ft) in height and spreading to about 45cm (18in), ***Liriope*** can also be used as an edging. There are varieties with variegated leaves like ***L. m.*** 'Gold-banded' and ***L. m.*** 'Variegata', but their foliage will scorch in hot sun.

Persicaria amplexicaulis (below) spreads quickly to make a dense, clumping thicket of lax stems carrying pokers of bright pink flowers in autumn. I like to see it among the hip-bearing branches of species roses like *Rosa glauca*. The cultivar *P. a.* 'Firetail' has more reddish tinted flowers than the species. Commonly called knotweed, it can be invasive, but is easily pulled out from where it is not wanted. It does best in moisture-retentive soil, in sun or part shade. *P. affinis* is the mat-forming, dwarf relative that makes tiny, intensely pink spikes in autumn; it looks great tumbling down a wall. *P. affinis* 'Darjeeling Red' is especially well coloured.

Nerine bowdenii (above) is an autumn-flowering bulb that makes a spectacular show when planted in bold masses. Each flowerhead is composed of about 8–10 individual blooms in bright fuchsia-pink. These top stiffly erect stems that are roughly 45cm (18in) tall. Like colchicums and crinums, the flowers of nerines appear before the foliage. When planting the bulbs, put them in open sandy soil in a sunny spot with their 'noses' just below the soil surface; they do best if they bake during summer. Once established, the colony should be left alone as they do not take kindly to being disturbed. Feed occasionally with a potash-rich plant food.

Phlox paniculata 'Norah Leigh' (above) is remarkable among the autumn-flowering cottage garden favourites for its cream variegated foliage. In fact, I feel the flowers get lost among the bright foliage, but then it does make a totally bright spot in the garden. Phlox do best in well-drained soil in sun and slowly increase to make sizeable clumps of sweetly scented flowers. Other phlox have plain green foliage but brilliant flower colour like *P. p.* 'Amethyst', with violet blue flowers; *P. p.* 'Bright Eyes', that has white flowers dotted pink in the centre; *P. p.* 'Fujiyama', pure white and prolific, and *P. p.* 'Blue Ice' which is almost, but not quite, blue.

Rudbeckia fulgida is an American prairie perennial, a robust plant that makes a pool of golden sunshine wherever it grows. In England, I grew the variety *R. f.* var. *deamii,* (above right) with *Stipa arundinacea,* because the orange autumn tint of the grass looked so well with the rudbeckia and reminded me, in a sideways sort of manner, of the prairies of my home state, Illinois. Rudbeckias are also half-hardy annuals, and the most outrageous is probably *R.* 'Kelvedon Star' with the base of each petal heavily blotched with chocolate brown. Another perennial that is equally strange is *R. occidentalis* 'Green Wizard' with big black central cones surrounded by bright green sepals – there are no petals on this aberration. *R.* 'Indian Summer' (above left) is a good simple flower with bright petals and a small central boss. Plant in well-drained soil in sun.

Salvia farinacea (above), or mealy sage, is a perennial sage that is usually grown as a half-hardy annual bedding plant. It is roughly 30cm (1ft) tall, and the rich purple-blue colour looks well with grasses and other late summer and early autumn plants. *S. f.* 'Strata' is a fine baby-blue cultivar. The seeds should be sown in spring and then pricked out to make plants for setting out in early summer. Other annual salvias are *S. splendens*, with *S. s.* 'Red Arrows' being especially vibrant, and *S. coccinea* 'Cherry Blossom', which is a pretty bicolour of pink and white. Plant in full sun in well-drained soil.

Perennial sages, apart from the ever-popular culinary herb, *S. officinalis*, are

Schizostylis coccinea 'Sunrise' (above), known commonly as the Kaffir lily, is a rhizomatous perennial that does best in full sun and well-drained soil that has had plenty of rotted compost added. It makes a terrific cut flower, so set out a row in the kitchen garden for indoor flower arrangements. It is one of those spiky plants that look well with cascading grasses or popping up from clumps of mounding or groundcovering herbs, such as *Salvia officinalis* 'Tricolor' with its purple and pink markings. *Schizostylis coccinea* 'Mrs Hegarty' is bright pink and vigorous and *S. c.* 'Viscountess Byng' has dependable autumn flowers in soft pink. *S. c.* 'Major' has large pink flowers.

also wonderfully decorative, and among the prettiest is the frost-tender Mexican sage bush, *S. leucantha* (above). It has heavily veined leaves that are silvery felted on the reverse but dark green above. The flower spikes also have some of the fuzziness of the foliage. It makes an open branching shrub reaching a height of about 60cm (2ft).

As a complete contrast, *S. verticillata* 'Purple Rain' (above centre) has finely cut leaves that give the whole plant an open lacy texture, above which the dark purple flower spikes float happily. Neither of these plants seem particularly hardy so it is probably advisable to take cuttings each summer to propagate for next year's planting. One other salvia worth growing for its showiness is *S. sclarea* var. *turkestanica*, which is biennial and seeds around freely. It makes a tall open branching plant with huge fuzzy leaves and large pale purple and white flower bracts. It is rather smelly – a common name being housemaid's armpit!

Sedum is unquestionably the autumn stalwart genus, which is not entirely fair, since these plants look good most of the year. They are hardy perennials that make clumps of fleshy stems with soft fleshy leaves and flower umbels variously tinted white to rosy pink. One of the very best is the small growing *S.* 'Bertram Anderson' (above), a small-leafed sort that makes a spreading clump of silvery green leaves that are tinted purplish-pink and topped with a mass of rosy-red flowers in late summer to early autumn.

S. middendorffianum var. *diffusum* (centre right) is unique for the multi-coloured flowerheads each plant carries; it has the fleshy foliage characteristic of the genus, but the flowers are its strong point. *S. spectabile* 'Iceberg' (far right) is one of the palest flowered, being a good clean white above fine green foliage. Both of these make medium-sized plants.

There are some sedums, like *S. telephium* 'Matrona' and *S. t.* 'Munstead Red' that have a deep red cast to the leaves; I think these are the best sorts, but I am partial to red and brown plants anyway. But they do make a solid mass against which lighter textured plants can be played to good effect. Their succulence means that sedums withstand drought really well and they enjoy a place in full sun. Too rich a soil makes them flaccid, so 'mean and lean' makes for the best results.

Solidago rugosa 'Fireworks' (above) is one of the prettiest goldenrods, sending out sprays of soft yellow blooms on arching stems, about 45–60cm (18–24in) long. It is incomparably delicate compared to its coarser sisters – a floral Cinderella. Goldenrods do make good garden plants – the ragged conical heads of sharp yellow make a good backdrop to stronger flower shapes and more demanding colours.

Solidago tends to spread like a thug, so do make sure you have the room and the will to control it. It grows just about anywhere, but full sun and free-draining soil are prefered.

Tricyrtis hirta (above), the toad lily, is a bit of a curiosity, and not one that I am wild about, although it is a good autumn-flowering plant; perhaps it doesn't have enough substance to suit my taste for showiness at this time of year. Anyway, there it is, the spotted starry flowers sit atop rigid stems that emerge from ground-hugging, spotted foliage. It probably looks best among ferns in a midsummer-night's dream-type setting of moist, warm soil in part shade.

Verbena bonariensis (above) has been one of my favourite plants ever since I saw it growing in naturalized masses in the remains of a Gertrude Jekyll garden, back in 1981. The area was a derelict iris garden on either side of a sunken path – the intention being that the iris blooms would be viewed at eye level. The verbena, with its whippy stems and glorious lavender-purple flowers, had just about taken over,

so all one could do was look down the throats of the tiny little trumpets, noting the orange speck at the base – knockout! I've been devoted ever since. A remnant of that memory exists in an iris bed I once planted with this verbena scattered amongst the rhizomes, so that at least after the irises faded, there was something to look at apart from the grey-green iris leaves. It will seed just about anywhere.

Zephyranthes candida (above) is the evergreen rain lily, of which I am becoming increasingly aware since it has naturalized in my front lawn in Texas. John Fairey, of the famous Peckerwood Garden Foundation near Houston, has been responsible for introducing a large selection of these plants from Mexico. There is a yellow-flowered species, *Z. citrina*, a purple tinted one, *Z. atamasco,* and *Z. grandiflora,* which is charmingly pink. In late summer and early autumn, the rain brings them into bloom after the dry dormant period of summer. They naturalize quickly in rich, well-drained soil and the ripe seedheads can be shaken like maracas to scatter the seed which will surely germinate. They are really only half-hardy although they will succeed in cool-climate gardens if given a sheltered spot.

Zinnia, like *Dahlia*, provides a wide range of flower colour and size and no autumn garden would be complete without a contribution from this genus. Native to the warm southwestern USA and Mexico, zinnias are half-hardy annuals and should be sown in the early spring to plant out after all hint of frost has left the garden. Shown here is *Z.* 'Chippendale' (above), and it is typical of the loose cheerful branching clumps that this annual will form. Deadhead regularly to keep in flower and plant in a well-drained soil in full sun for the very best flowers.

PICTURE ACKNOWLEDGEMENTS

I am very grateful to the following garden owners and designers for allowing me to take pictures and for providing invaluable assistance and support (L=left; C=centre; R=right; T=top; B=bottom): Abbey Dore Garden, Herefordshire, Charis Ward 22–23, 26, 32–33, 43, 71, 126L, 142, 144C, 146, 147R; Bath Botanic Gardens, Somerset 12–13, 18–19, 38, 133T; Batsford Arboretum, Gloucestershire 14, 118R; Le Berquerie, Varengeville-sur-Mer, Normandy, France, Mark Brown 62, 64, 84R, 134C, 149LB, 158L; Beth Chatto Gardens, Essex, Beth Chatto 50, 52, 68, 132R, 134R, 135T, 140C/front cover, 141R, 143R, 150RB, 150RT, 156L; Bois des Moutiers, Varengeville-sur-Mer, Normandy, France, Mme Mary Mallet 65, 108–109, 124L; Castelnau, Barnes, London, Gay Search, Designer Dan Pearson 2–3, 135B; Chiltern Road, Wendover, Bucks, Jo Chatterton 144L; Clos Normand, Varengeville-sur-Mer, Normandy, France, Mme Constance Kargére 80, 124C; Cotswold Garden Flowers, Worcestershire, Bob Brown 21, 56, 138; The Dingle, Welshpool, Powys, Roy and Barbara Joseph 4, 15, 24, 25, 111, 116–117, 120L, 121R, 121L, 122L, 122R, 125R, 126–127, 128B, 134L, 140L, 145B; Dinmore Manor, Herefordshire, R.G. Murray 18L; Dolwen, Llanrhaeadr, Powys, Frances Denby 5/139R/back cover, 34; The Old Vicarage, East Ruston, Norfolk, Alan Gray and Graham Robeson 7, 36–37, 100–101, 101, 106, 112, 114, 115, 124–125, 129R, 141L; Eastgrove Cottage Garden, Worcestershire, Malcolm and Carol Skinner 95, 127C, 151L, 162L; Elsing Hall, Norfolk, Shirley and David Cargill 130L; Great Dixter, East Sussex, Christopher Lloyd 1/155C, 41, 46, 66–67, 70, 81, 84L, 93, 102–103, 120C, 137, 147CB, 147CT, 150L, 152C, 152–153, 153T, 155R, 157RB, 157L, 160L, 161LB, 161R, 164–165, 164L, 165R; Green Farm Plants, Hampshire, J. Coke 45, 57, 97; Hergest Croft, Herefordshire, W.L and R.A. Banks 8, 118L; The Hiller Garden, Worcestershire, Designer Bob Brown 9, 58, 59, 63, 79, 110, 144R, 149LT, 154R, 160R, 161LT, 162R, 163L; Holker Hall, Cumbria, Lord and Lady Cavendish 19R, 122C, 128T; Leila Cabot Perry Garden, Museum of American Impressionism, Giverny, France, Designer Mark Brown 60–61; The Lodge, Sussex, Mr and Mrs Upton 90–91; Merriments, East Sussex, Mark Buchele 76–77, 145T; Picton Garden, Herefordshire, Paul Picton 156R, 143L; Powis Castle, Powys, National Trust 6–7, 130R; RHS Gardens, Wisley 55, 117, 131, 136, 148LB, 151CB, 151RT, 153B, 157C, 163C; Stockton Bury, Herefordshire, Raymond Treasure and Gordon Fenn 30, 121C; Sycamore Barn, Norfolk, Ethne Clarke 96; Upper Mill Cottage, Kent, David and Mavis Seeney 10–11, 13, 51, 87, 89, 107, 132CB, 133B, 155L, 155C, 158R, 164C; Valley Gardens (Windsor Great Park), Surrey 119, 120R, 123T, 123B, 125C, 140R; Waterperry Gardens, Oxfordshire 39, 44–45, 82, 83, 98, 129L, 129C, 139L, 148LT, 149R; West Dean Gardens, West Sussex 47, 72–73, 73, 74, 75, 94, 132CT, 159L, 165C; White Windows, Hampshire, Jane Sterndale-Bennett 31, 42, 127R, 148R, 152L, 156C, 159R, 160C, 162C, 163R.

In addition to the above I would like to thank Fergus Garrett, Mark Flanagan, Ruth and Sam Buckley, Jim Buckland and Sarah Wain for their help with this project and Ethne Clarke for her faith in it.

Jonathan Buckley

BIBLIOGRAPHY

Chatto, Beth, *The Green Tapestry*, Harper Collins, 1989

Clarke, Ethne, *The Art of the Kitchen Garden*, Michael Joseph, 1988

Hidcote: the Making of a Garden, Michael Joseph, 1989

Herb Garden Design, Frances Lincoln, 1995

Leaf, Bark and Berry, David & Charles, 1996

Fish, Margery, *A Flower for Every Day*, Faber, 1965

Larkcom, Joy, *Creative Vegetable Gardening*, Mitchell Beazley, 1997

Ogden, Scott, *Gardening Success with Difficult Soils (Limestone, Alkaline Clay and Caliche)*, Taylor, 1992

Rix, Marytn and Roger Phillips, *Shrubs*, Pan, 1989; *Perennials,* vol. 1 & 2, Pan, 1991

Robinson, William, *The English Flower Garden*, John Murray, 1883

The Wild Garden, John Murray, 1870

INDEX

Page numbers in *italics* refer to picture captions. Those entries that fall within pages 117-165 (*Great Autumn Plants*) and which are in *italics* indicate that a text reference is accompanied by a picture.